texts : Nathalie Louveau, Monique Subra-Jourdain

illustrations : Nathalie Louveau

CARCASSONNE BASTIDE,
CARCASSONNE CITÉ

Thanking Claude Marquié and Philippe Satgé for their help with the realization of the present work.

maquette : Mathieu Subra – traduction : Guillaume Subra

© 2006 ÉDITIONS DU CABARDÈS,11610 Ventenac-Cabardès
Dépôt légal, 2ᵉ trimestre 2006. ISBN 2-9526802-0-5
Impression FRANCE QUERCY, Cahors

LA CITÉ

• 6th CENTURY BC

BUILDING OF THE «OPPIDUM DE CARCASO», ON THE COMMERCIAL ROUTE BETWEEN THE ATLANTIC OCEAN AND THE MEDITERRANEAN SEA. IT OVERLOOKS THE FORT ON THE RIVER.

• GALLO-ROMAN TIME

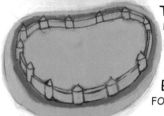

THE CITÉ BECOMES AN URBAN CENTRE.

DURING THE 5th CENTURY, THE GALLO-ROMANS SHELTER THEMSELVES FROM THE BARBARIAN ATTACKS IN A FORTIFIED WALL.

• FEUDAL TIME

ARRIVAL OF THE VISIGOTHS, WHO REINFORCE THE WALL, THEN OF THE MOORS AND THE FRANKS, AND FINALLY DURING THE 11th AND 12th CENTURIES, OF THE DYNASTY OF THE TRENCAVEL. AT THAT TIME, THERE IS STILL ONLY ONE WALL.

TWO EXTERIOR SUBURBS GROW ATTACHED TO THE WALLS OF THE CITÉ.

• ROYAL TIME

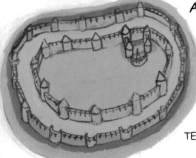

AFTER THE ALBIGENSIAN CRUSADE, THE CITÉ BECOMES A ROYAL FORTRESS DEFENDING THE BORDER BETWEEN FRANCE AND SPAIN. A SECOND WALL IS ERECTED. THE BASTIDE SAINT-LOUIS WAS BUILT IN 1260, ON THE OTHER SIDE OF THE RIVER AUDE. FROM THEN ON, THE BASTIDE DEVELOPS QUICKLY, WHEREAS THE CITÉ IS ONLY INHABITED BY THE POOREST.

chivalry tournaments

28

thé

23

18

lices hautes (upper lists)

basilique Saint Naze

29

musée "Mémoires Moyen-Âge"

• CONTEMPORARY TIME

WITH THE 19th CENTURY, THE CITÉ, IN DECAY, IS STILL INHABITED. VIOLLET-LE-D YEAR 1853, START ITS RESTORATION. THE CITÉ IS TODAY INHABITED BY A HUNDRED SIDENTS, AND WAS ADDED TO THE UNESCO LIST OF WORLD HERITAGE IN 1997.

2

PLAN

RUE DE LA BARBACANE

MONTÉE D'AUDE

Eglise St Gimer

the Château Comtal

inner wall

outer wall

el de Cité

Porte d'Aude

Musée de la chevalerie

RUE PORTE D'AUDE

VT-LOUIS

14

10 **12**

16

place du château

place du Grand Puits

lices basses (lower lists)

RUE TRENCAVEL

6

2

mall well

RUE CRCS-MAYREVIELLE

place Marcou

25

DU PLÔ

RUE DU GRAND PUITS

tourism information centre

26

Porte Narbonnaise

drawbridge

4

moat

RUE NADAUD

: PAGE REFERENCES

3

THE PORTE NARBONNAISE IS THE MAIN ENTRANCE TO THE CITÉ. IT IS ACCESSIBLE VIA THE DRAWBRIDGE, WHICH WOULD BE RAISED UP WHEN THE TOWN WAS UNDER SIEGE.

LOOKING UP, YOU WILL SEE THE GROOVES THAT HELD THE PORTCULLIS (A WOODEN GRID FACED WITH IRON THAT WOULD BE LOWERED FROM THE UPPER STORY) AND MACHICOLATION (OPENINGS IN THE CEILING ALLOWING DEFENDERS TO ATTACK ENEMIES FROM ABOVE).

the tours narbonnaises, the two sentinels keeping an eye over the Cité

meurtrière

crenel (opening)

merlon (square saw-teeth)

THE PORTE NARBONNAISE WAS QUITE VULNERABLE, AS IT WAS AT GROUND LEVEL.

TO MAKE UP FOR THIS, THE TOWERS AND THE DRAWBRIDGE WERE NOT ALIGNED.

THAT WAY, THE ATTACKERS COULD NOT STEP BACK AND USE A BATTERING RAM.

moat (that was never filled with water)

The train goes around the Cité, every between the 1st of May and the 30th of S

tour du Tréseau

tour du Moulin du Connétable

inner wall

Raise your nose and check the machicolation of the tours narbonnaises

The barouche through the lists

IF YOU'RE NOT MUCH INTO WALKING, CONSIDER THE BAROUCHES AND THE TRAIN. BOTH WILL GIVE A UNIQUE PERSPECTIVE OF THE CITÉ.

play ring

drawbridge

Check what's written underneath: SUM CARCAS, which means "I am Carcas" in latin. The bust represents Dame Carcas, who according to the legend gave her name to the town.

Dame Carcas

I wonder who this is ... and what she's doing there?!

cobbles

The Cité has been on the UNESCO list of World Heritage since 1997.

departure of the train

5

The rue Cros-Mayrevielle is a very typical mediaeval street. It is narrow, and you can find on either side half-timbered houses, replicas of what would have been seen in the Middle Age. Back then, streets were rather dirty and dark. At dusk, bells would sound to announce the curfew. Lanterns and candles would be blown out: accidents with fire were frequent in the wood-built houses of the time.

Do step on a few feet and elbow your way in if you feel the urge to count the towers of the Cité! There are 52 of the

AN-PIERRE CROS-MAYREVIELLE WAS BORN NEAR THE WALLS OF THE
É, RUE TRIVALLE. AT THE AGE OF 6, HE WITNESSED THE START OF THE DESTRUCTION OF THE
CITADEL. IT WAS THEN USED AS A GRAVEL-PIT TO BUILD HOUSING IN THE LOW TOWN. AP-
NTED INSPECTOR OF THE HISTORICAL MONUMENTS, HE DEFENDED THE PRESTIGE OF THE CITÉ.
OLLET-LE-DUC, ARCHITECT, WAS SENT TO START THE RESTORATION IN 1853.

BUST OF JEAN-PIERRE CROS-MAYREVIELLE
(1810 - 1876)

LE CHÂTEAU COMTAL

tour du Moulin d'Avar

watch tower

donjon

early palace against the interior wall

inner wall

court of honor

holes for the hoard

moat

bridge

seal of Trencavel

entrance of the castle

WAAAAH! That sounds like good fun!

outer wall

inner wall

moat

① ③

castle of Trencavel

bridge

② fortifications added by Louis IX

MAP OF THE CHÂTEAU COMTAL

THE BUILDING WHICH ACCOMMODATED THE STEWAR WAS STARTED IN THE 12ᵗʰ CENTURY BY THE VISCOU OF TRENCAVEL, AND WAS FINISHED IN THE 13ᵗʰ CEN TURY UNDER LOUIS IX.

ONE OF THE FACADES OF THE CASTLE IS PART OF TH FIRST FORTIFICATION WALLS. DOWN FROM THE FA CADE WAS A DEFENSIVE CONSTRUCTION: the BARBA CANE D'AUDE ❶, (DISMANTLED TODAY). IT PROTECTE BOTH THE CASTLE AND THE WESTERN ENTRANCE OF CITÉ : the PORTE D'AUDE.

AFTER YOU'VE GONE THROUGH THE FIRST DOOR OF THE CASTLE ❷ TAKE THE BRIDGE WHICH W TAKE YOU TO THE SECOND ENTRANCE. IT IS VERY NARROW: IT ONLY ALLOWS ONE OR TWO PERSON TO CROSS AT A TIME, MAKING IT A LOT EASIER TO DEFEND! THIS ENTRANCE IS WELL PROTECTED WITH MACHICOLATION AND WOODEN DOOR PANELS.

THE ENTRANCE FOR HORSES ❸ WAS ALSO THE MAIN ENTRANCE FOR THE CASTLE AT THE TIME OF THE TRENCAVEL FAMILY.

tour de la Chapelle

tour Pinte

inner wall

wooden hoardings

AT THE ENTRANCE OF THE CASTLE, LOOK UP AND CHECK THE WOODEN CONSTRUCTIONS: THEY ARE CALLED HOARDINGS. THESE ARE ACTUALLY REPLICAS. THEY WOULD BE INSTALLED EVERYWHERE ON THE FORTIFICATIONS AGAINST POTENTIAL INVASIONS. PLACED ABOVE THE WALLS, THE HOLES IN THE WALLS WERE USED TO SUPPORT THEM. PROJECTILES WOULD THEN BE THROWN AT THE ENEMY: STONES, TILES, SAND, BOILING WATER, MELTED LEAD, PITCH...

THE WOODEN HOARDINGS

gallery

openwork floor

...HIS WALKWAY WAS USED TO DEPLOY ...D SUPPLY SOLDIERS WITH AMMU- TIONS WHILE KEEPING THEM SAFE ...OM ENEMY MISSILES.

...ODAY, THE ENTRANCE OF THE CASTLE IS ...STEGED BY NOTHING MORE DEADLY THAN A ...VELY ARRAY OF STREET ARTIST. ...HEY LIVEN UP THE CITÉ, ENTERTAINING ...UNGSTERS OF ALL AGES.

THEATRE WYNFYD

L'HERBE FOLLE

LE CHÂTEAU COMTAL

tour de la Poudre

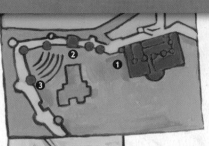

GUIDED VISIT OF THE WALL-WALK

YOU ARE NOW IN THE INNER WARD OF THE CHÂTEAU DU VICOMTE. IF YOU CHOOSE TO TAKE THE **45** MINUTES TOUR, FOLLOW THE TOUR GUIDE! HE WILL TAKE YOU UP THE WALL-WALK.

the gui

HE WILL SHOW YOU:

THE TOUR DE JUSTICE ❶, WHERE THE INQUISITION WOULD KEEP ITS ARCHIVES SAFE.

FURTHER ALONG, FROM THE OPENWORK ROMAN WINDOWS, LOOK OUTSIDE: A SMALL CONSTRUCTION ABOVE THE GATE, CALLED BRETASCHE OR BOX MACHICOLATION, WAS USED TO THROW PROJECTILES ON THE ENEMIES BLOCKED BY THE DOOR.

our two her

bretasche

STILL FURTHER ❷ IS THE TOUR CARRÉE DE L'ÉVEQUE, WHICH VIOLLET-LE-DUC USED AS AN OFFICE.

ITS ORIGINALITY LAYS IN THAT IT GOES ACROSS THE ALLURE: IT RESTS ON THE INNER SIDE OF ONE WALL, AND ON THE OUTER SIDE OF THE OTHER.

AT THE CORNERS OF THIS TOWER, SMALL CONSTRUCTIONS ARE OVERHANGING, FOR PROTECTION. THAT WAY, NO BLIND SPOT!

bartiz

> *And on we go, don't even try to lift the balls, they are sealed to the ground!*

ON THE TOUR MI PADRE ❸ ARE WOODEN SHUTTERS, ALLOWING THE BREEZE TO CIRCULATE WHILE PROTECTING FROM SHOTS. THE VIEW ON THE BASILIQUE SAINT-NAZAIRE FROM THERE IS JUST SUPERB. CHECK THE OPEN AIR THEATRE TOO!

shutte

INSIDE THE CASTLE

INSIDE THE CHATEAU COMTAL IS A 12th CENTURY FRESCO. IT REPRESENTS THE EXPLOITS OF THE LORDS DURING THE CRUSADES IN SPAIN AND AGAINST THE MOORS.

ALSO, ON THE FIRST FLOOR IS THE LAPIDARY STORE. THE WORD LAPIDARY REFERS TO OBJECTS MADE OF STONE: SCULPTURES, STONE, PIECES OF ARCHITECTU-RE... THEY ALL DATE FROM DIFFERENT TIMES.

FRESCO, END OF THE 12TH C.

STONES

FOUNTAIN OF ABLUTION, 12TH C.

THE VIRGIN AND CHILD

If I tickle him, will it wake him up?

Don't be silly!

RECUMBENT STATUE OF A KNIGHT, 13TH C.

11

tour des Casernes

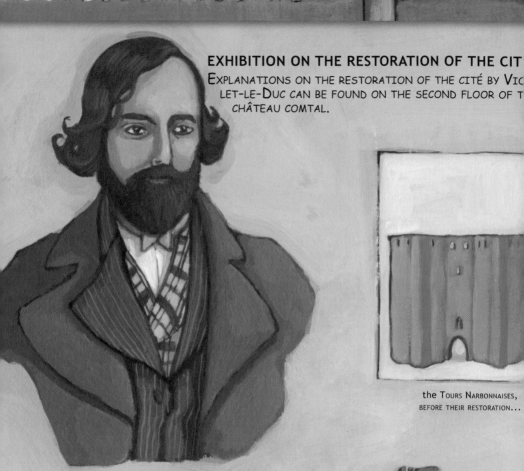

EXHIBITION ON THE RESTORATION OF THE CIT
EXPLANATIONS ON THE RESTORATION OF THE CITÉ BY VIO LET-LE-DUC CAN BE FOUND ON THE SECOND FLOOR OF T CHÂTEAU COMTAL.

the TOURS NARBONNAISES, BEFORE THEIR RESTORATION...

EUGÈNE VIOLLET-LE-DUC (1814-1879)

The Tour Saint-Nazaire was almost destroyed when Viollet-le-Duc started his restoration project!

THE TOUR SAINT-NAZAIRE

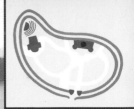

AT THE BEGINNING OF THE 19th CENTURY, THE CITÉ, ALTHOUGH STILL INHABITED,
[I]S IN RUINS.

[JEA]N-PIERRE CROS MAYREVIELLE CALLED FOR PROSPER MÉRIMÉE, DIRECTOR OF THE HISTO-
[RIC]AL MONUMENTS DEPARTMENT. THE LATTER GAVE TO VIOLLET-LE-DUC THE RESPONSABILITY
[OF T]HE RESTORATION OF THE BASILIQUE SAINT-NAZAIRE, AND LATER OF THE CITÉ. IN 1853,
[THE] RESTORATION OF THE CITÉ BEGINS, STARTING WITH PART OF THE WALLS AND THE TOURS

[CON]STITUTION BY VIOLLET LE DUC...   PROJECT OF RESTORATION...   TODAY, IN THEIR FINAL STATE

[W]ITH THE DRAWINGS OF VIOLLET-LE-DUC, ALONGSIDE TO THE PHOTOS
[OF] THE TIME, WE CAN GET A CLEAR IDEA OF HOW THE RESTORATION
[TO]OK PLACE.

[AB]OUT 15% OF THE CITÉ HAS BEEN REBUILT. THE UPPER PARTS OF THE
[TO]WERS WERE THE CENTRE OF PARTICULAR CARE. THE WORKS CONTINUED
[AF]TER VIOLLET-LE-DUC'S DEATH. THEY ENDED IN 1911.

Waaah!
Wish I had
my lego
with me to play
in there...

It'd be just
like a forgotten
city!

IT TOOK LOUIS LACOMBE OVER THIRTY YEARS TO ACCOMPLISH THIS GIGANTIC MODEL OF THE CITÉ.

LA PORTE D'AUDE

tour de Justice

THE MUSÉE DE LA CHEVALERIE

THE MUSÉE DE LA CHEVALERIE IS NEARBY THE PORTE D'AUDE IN THE OLD HOUSE OF THE INQUISITION.

THIS MUSEUM PRESENTS YOU WITH VARIOUS REPRODUCTION. OF MIDDLE AGES' WEAPONS, ARMOURS, TAPESTRIES, AND COSTUMES.

two-handed sword

helm of the Black Prince (son of the king of England, he destroyed the down town part of Carcassonne in 1355)

jousting helm 16th c.

crossbow

an armor could weight up to 50 kg

THE OWNER OF THIS SMALL MUSEUM SOMETIMES SHOWS THE DIFFERENT WAYS OF WIELDING OF A SWORD.

Wow, that's pretty heavy!

The tapestries are probably the best account we have of the lives of the lords!

r Wisigothe   tour ronde de   tour carrée de
l'Evêque   l'Evêque

inner wall

E LIFE OF LORDS AND KNIGHTS IN THE MIDDLE AGES

RING THE SECOND HALF OF THE 11th CENTURY, THE CHURCH IMPOSED RELIGIOUS MORALE
D RULES FOR THE CODE OF CHIVALRY: PROTECTION OF THE POOR ONES, OF THE ORPHANS AND
DOWS, LOYALTY, FIDELITY AND BRAVERY. THE LIFE OF THE LORDS AND KNIGHTS WAS HENCE
MPOSED OF HUNTING, BANQUETS, MUSIC, WARS AND CRUSADES...

off crusading

the hunting

IVALRY IS A FEUDAL INSTITUTION
THERING COMBATANTS ON HORSES.
TER A LONG
PARATION,
CESS TO
IVALRY WAS
HIEVED WITH
E CEREMONY
THE DUB-
IG.

jousts

musicians

jugglers

THE LIFE OF VILLEINS IN THE MIDDLE AGES

> This is the deepest well of the Cité!

> I can't see anything in there! Thank God it's protected, I wouldn't want to fall down!

NEAR THE CHATEAU COMTAL, IS THE PLACE DU GRAND PUITS (PLACE OF THE BIG WELL).

IT DATES BACK FROM TH 14th CENTURY, AND IS ALMOST 40 METRES DEEP.

THE TWO PILLARS US TO SUPPORT A SYSTEM ALLOWING DIFFERENT PEOPLE TO GET WATER AT THE SAME TIME.

DURING THE MIDDLE AGES, THERE WAS NO RUNNING WATER AND HOUSES WERE NOT EQUIPPED WITH TAPS. GETTING WATER WAS THUS IMPORTANT, AS WE CAN'T LIVE WITHOUT IT.

washerwome

VILLAGES WERE NOT BUILLT AT RANDOM. PEOPLE OFTEN ESTABLISHED SETTLEMENTS NEAR RIVERS OR SPRINGS. WOOD WAS ALSO NECESSARY FOR HEATING AND COOKING, AND STONES FOR THE BUILDING OF HOUSES.

> It is said that Visigoths had the treasure of Rome in this well. When we went to look for it, we only found a few arrows and medals. What a disappointment!

tour Nipadre

tour du Moulin du Midi

tour Porte St Nazaire

inner wall

the dyers

in the vineyard

a ploughing peasant

17

YOU LOOK UP, YOU'LL DISCOVER MONSTROUS FIGURES ON THE WALL, ALL AROUND THE BASI- A. THESE ARE MODILLONS AND GARGOYLES.

DILLONS ARE PLACED ON THE FACADE, ABOVE THE ENTRANCE GATE.

THE OTHER HAND, GARGOYLES ARE TO BE FOUND ALL AROUND THE BASILICA.

EY SERVE AS GUTTERS TO THE BASI- A, KEEPING THE WATER AWAY FROM WALLS.

Gargoyle? The name comes from the gurgling sound it makes when it rains!

That one, probably gurgles louder ...

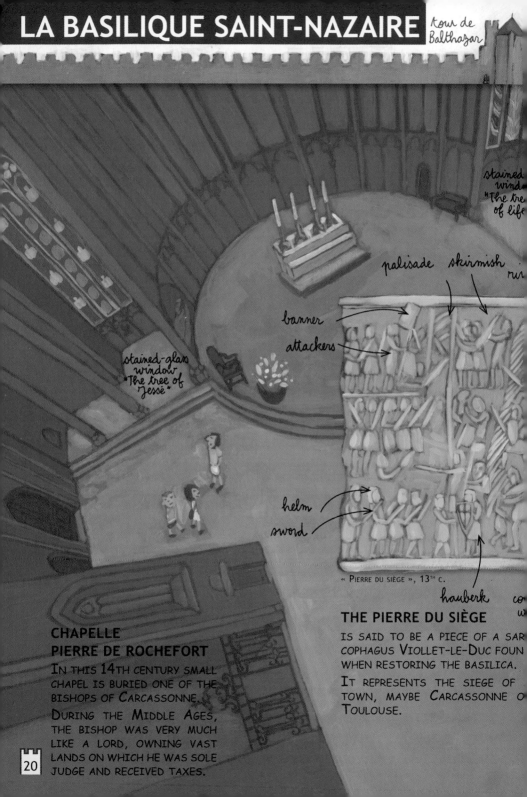

tour de Balthazar

stained window "The tree of life"

palisade   skirmish   ru

banner

attackers

stained-glass window "The tree of Jessé"

helm

sword

« PIERRE DU SIÈGE », 13TH C.

hauberk   co   w

THE PIERRE DU SIÈGE

IS SAID TO BE A PIECE OF A SAR COPHAGUS VIOLLET-LE-DUC FOUN WHEN RESTORING THE BASILICA.

IT REPRESENTS THE SIEGE OF TOWN, MAYBE CARCASSONNE O TOULOUSE.

CHAPELLE PIERRE DE ROCHEFORT

IN THIS 14TH CENTURY SMALL CHAPEL IS BURIED ONE OF THE BISHOPS OF CARCASSONNE.

DURING THE MIDDLE AGES, THE BISHOP WAS VERY MUCH LIKE A LORD, OWNING VAST LANDS ON WHICH HE WAS SOLE JUDGE AND RECEIVED TAXES.

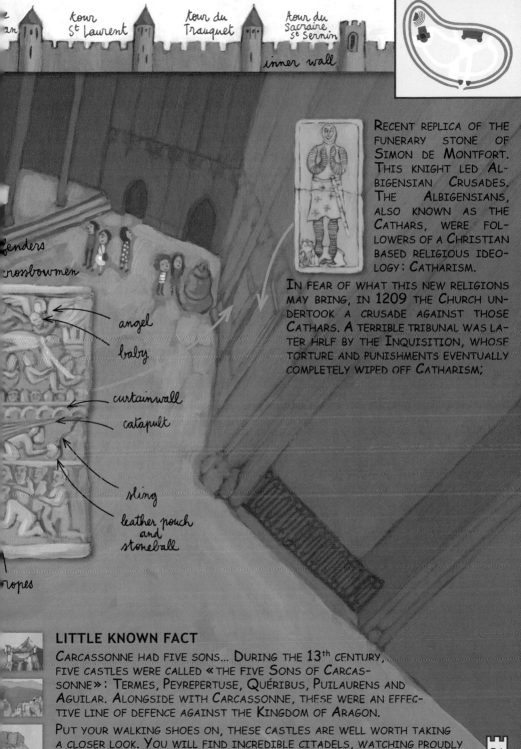

tour
St Laurent

tour du
Trauquet

tour du
Sacraire
St Sernin

inner wall

RECENT REPLICA OF THE FUNERARY STONE OF SIMON DE MONTFORT. THIS KNIGHT LED ALBIGENSIAN CRUSADES. THE ALBIGENSIANS, ALSO KNOWN AS THE CATHARS, WERE FOLLOWERS OF A CHRISTIAN BASED RELIGIOUS IDEOLOGY: CATHARISM.

IN FEAR OF WHAT THIS NEW RELIGIONS MAY BRING, IN 1209 THE CHURCH UNDERTOOK A CRUSADE AGAINST THOSE CATHARS. A TERRIBLE TRIBUNAL WAS LATER HRLF BY THE INQUISITION, WHOSE TORTURE AND PUNISHMENTS EVENTUALLY COMPLETELY WIPED OFF CATHARISM;

defenders
crossbowmen

angel

baby

curtainwall

catapult

sling

leather pouch
and
stoneball

ropes

LITTLE KNOWN FACT

CARCASSONNE HAD FIVE SONS... DURING THE 13th CENTURY, FIVE CASTLES WERE CALLED « THE FIVE SONS OF CARCASSONNE »: TERMES, PEYREPERTUSE, QUÉRIBUS, PUILAURENS AND AGUILAR. ALONGSIDE WITH CARCASSONNE, THESE WERE AN EFFECTIVE LINE OF DEFENCE AGAINST THE KINGDOM OF ARAGON.

PUT YOUR WALKING SHOES ON, THESE CASTLES ARE WELL WORTH TAKING A CLOSER LOOK. YOU WILL FIND INCREDIBLE CITADELS, WATCHING PROUDLY FROM THEIR MOUNTAIN PEAKS.

barbacane
St Louis

THE MUSÉE DE L'ÉCOLE

IN THE OLD DAYS, PURPLE INK AND QUILL PE
WERE USED TO WRITE. THE MUSÉE DE L'ÉCO
IS A FAITHFUL REPLICA OF WHAT A CLASS W
LIKE. THERE IS EVEN A WRITING WORKSH
WHERE YOU'LL GET A CHANCE TO EXPERIME
QUILLS!

NEED A REST? AROUND THE THEATRE, AND
JUST ABOUT EVERYWHERE IN THE CITÉ, ARE
REFRESHMENT SPOTS WHERE YOU CAN HAVE A
NICE TIME IN THE SHADE.

THE OPEN AIR THEATRE

THE THEATRE WAS BUILT AT THE BEGINNING OF THE 20th CENTURY, IN 1908, WHERE A VINEYARD WAS. BEFORE THAT, JUST NEARBY WAS THE CLOISTER OF THE BASILIQUE SAINT-NAZAIRE.

TODAY, THE THEATRE HOSTS AN IMPORTANT FESTIVAL IN JULY AND PERFORMANCES IN AUGUST.

IT IS SO NICE TO SIT AND ENJOY A SHOW OUTSIDE AFTER A LONG AND HOT DAY, WHEN THE TEMPERATURE FINALLY DROPS!

wall-walk on which the guide will take you for the guided visit of the Château Comtal

tour Mipadre

tour de Cahuzac

the seats

The first performance was on July the 26th, 1908. The seats were on the same level at that time, so that most of the 5000 spectators could see nothing from their chairs! Hats had to be forbidden. Such a shame, they must have been such pretty sight!

tour de moreti

tour de la glacière

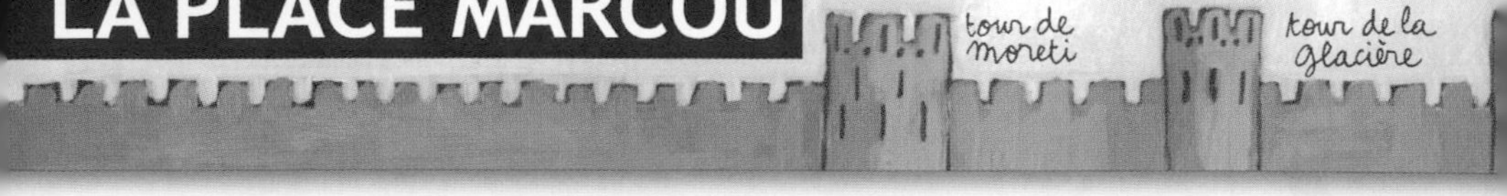

THE CASSOULET

WHAT'S FOR DINNER THEN? GIVE A TRY TO THE TYPICAL DISH OF THE REGION, T CASSOULET! YOU WILL FIND IT IN THE CITÉ, BUT ALSO IN ALL THE RESTAURANTS THE BASTIDE.

WHAT IS A CASSOULET?

THE DISH IS COOKED IN A LARGE CLAY CALLED A CASSOLE. ITS V SHAPE ALLOWS GOOD THOROUGH COOKING. IT USED TO BE DONE AT THE BREAD MAKER'S.

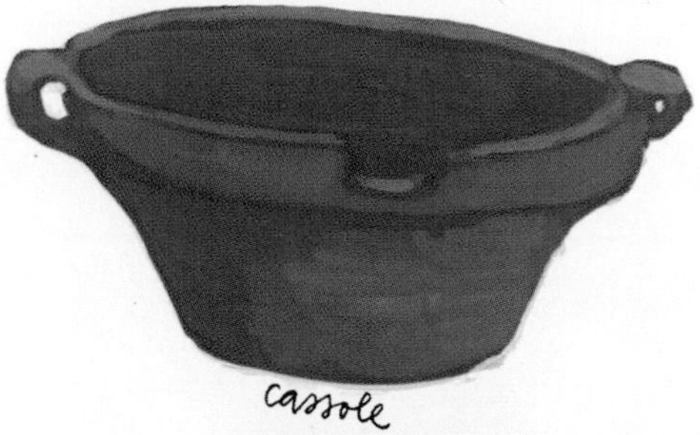

cassole

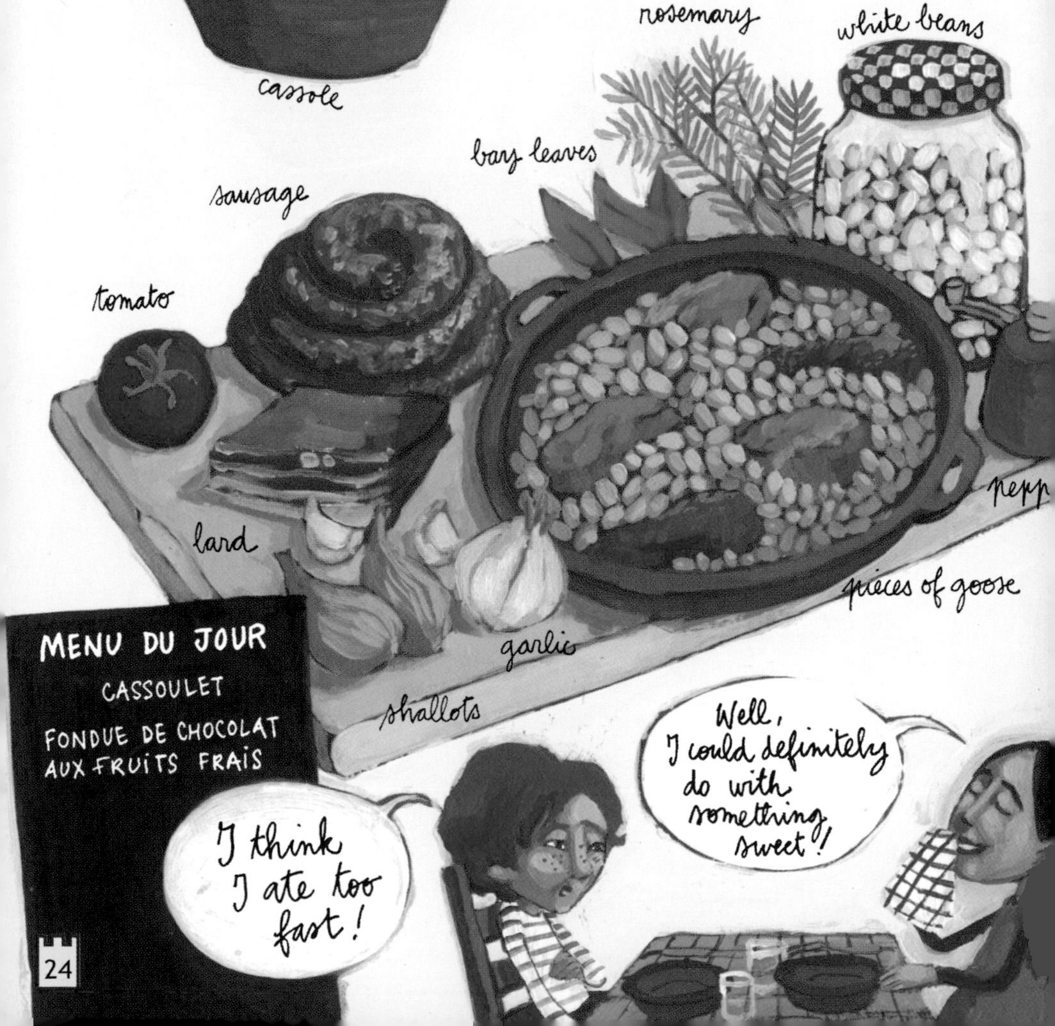

rosemary

white beans

bay leaves

sausage

tomato

lard

garlic

shallots

pepp

pieces of goose

I think I ate too fast!

Well, I could definitely do with something sweet!

tour de la
te Rouge

tour du
Petit Canisson

tour du
Grand Canisson

outer wall

THE PLACE MARCOU

ACCORDING TO THE SEASON, THE CITÉ CHANGES
DRASTICALLY. IT MAKES SUCH A DIFFERENCE FOR
ITS INHABITANTS!

SUMMER

WINTER

25

LES LICES

tour du Grand Burlas

tour d'Ourliac

tour St Martin

THE LISTS CORRESPOND TO THE SPACE SITU-
TED BETWEEN THE INNER WALL AND THE OUT-
WALL. IT GOES ALL AROUND THE CITÉ.

inner wall

tour des Prisons

tour du Castera

tour de la Vade

outter wall

the lists

LOOK CAREFULLY AT THE INNER WALL AND ITS
TOWERS. THERE ARE HINTS OF THE DIFFERENT
TIMES OF THE CONSTRUCTION, OF THE CONSO-
LIDATION AND RESTORATION OF THE CITÉ.

Hey! Check this out!
Some towers have a stream
of red bricks! The roofs are not
always similar, and the apertures
have different shapes! Each tower
has its story to tell.

roof of U shap tiles

restoration (Viollet-le-Du 19th c.)

small additi (gallo-roma times, 5th c

gallo-roman (reinforced dur the 13th c.)

TOUR DE LA CHARPENTIÈRE

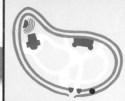

Barbacane
Crémade

tour
Cautière

outer wall

A SARACEN WOMAN, KNOWN AS DAME CARCAS, DEFENDED THE CITÉ WITH HER SOLDIERS AGAINST CHARLEMAGNE, EMPEROR OF THE FRANCS.

DAME CARCAS GRADUALLY LOST ALL OF HER ARMY. SHE THEN THOUGHT OF A CUNNING PLAN.

ALL OVER THE WALLS, SHE PUT SCARECROWS. CHARLEMAGNE THUS THOUGHT THAT THE SOLDIERS WERE STILL NUMEROUS TO DEFEND THE CITÉ.

BEING SHORT OF SUPPLY, SHE GATHERED ALL THE REMAINING WHEAT AND FED IT TO THE LAST PIG. AFTER WHAT THE OVERFED PIG WAS THROWN OVER THE WALLS.

THE PIG BURST UPON LANDING, SHOWING HOW MUCH FOOD WAS IN IT. CHARLEMAGNE THOUGHT THAT THE TOWN WAS STILL RICH AND WELL GUARDED.

DISCOURAGED, HE DECIDED TO LIFT THE SIEGE. BELLS OF THE CITÉ RANG TO DECLARE STATE OF PEACE.

UPON WHICH THE EMPEROR WAS TOLD: « DAME CARCAS SONNE* ! » (*FRENCH FOR RINGS THE BELLS).

HENCE, IT IS SAID, THE NAME OF CARCASSONNE !

restoration (Viollet-le-Duc 19th c.)

gothic window

small addition (gallo-roman times 5th c)

bricks

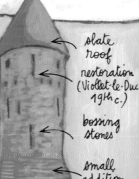

slate roof

restoration (Viollet-le-Duc 19th c.)

bossing stones

small addition (gallo-roman times 5th c.)

roof of flat tiles

wood-shringled roof

bossing stones (end 13th c.)

TOUR DU SACRAIRE SAINT-SERNIN

TOUR DU CASTÉRA

TOUR CARRÉE DE L'EVÊQUE

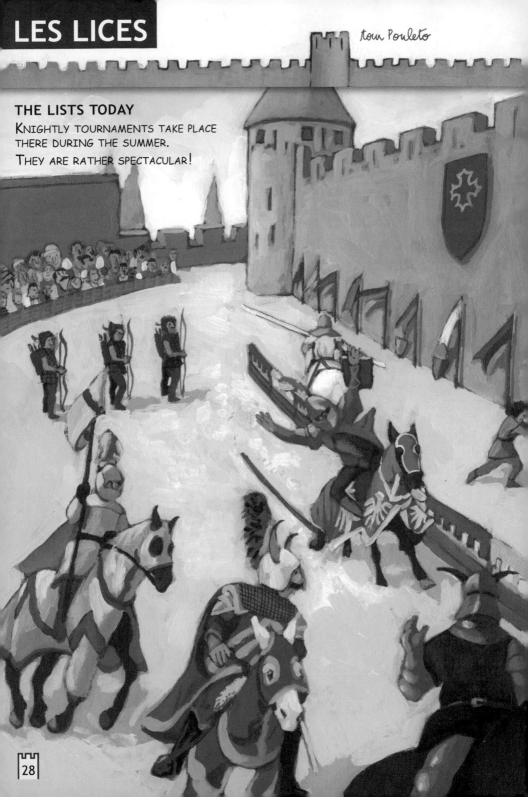

tour de la Vade

tour de la Peyre

outter wall

THE LISTS IN THE BEGINNING OF THE 19TH C.

WALKING DOWN THE LISTS, TAKE A CLOSE LOOK AT THE INNER WALL. AT SOME PLACES, TRACES CAN STILL BE FOUND OF HOUSES BUILT AGAINST THE WALL. THEY ACCOMMODATED THE WORKERS OF THE TOWN AS WELL AS THE WEAVERS. THE HOUSES THEMSELVES WERE IN A RATHER POOR STATE AND WERE DESTROYED DURING THE RESTORATION OF THE CITÉ.

tour de Davejean

tour St Laurent

tour du Trauquet

tours Narbonnaises

the lists of the Cité in 19th century

So, Holmes, finding any traces of the houses yet?

Still looking!

HISTOIRE DE LA CITÉ

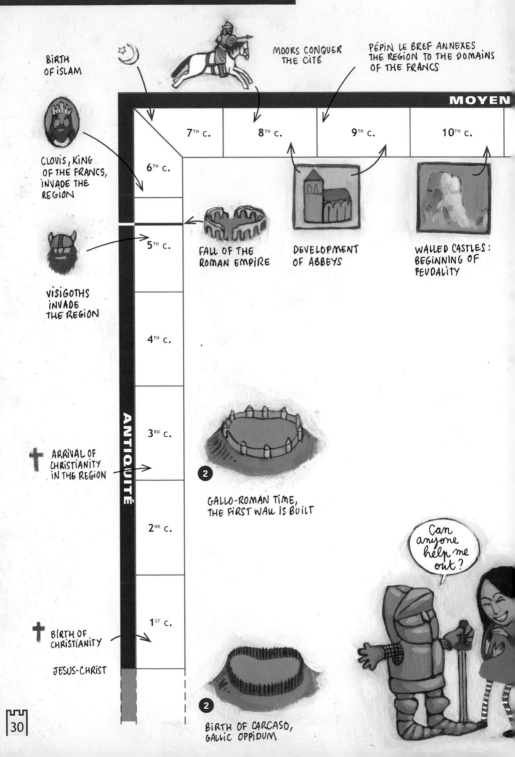

BIRTH OF ISLAM

MOORS CONQUER THE CITÉ

PÉPIN LE BREF ANNEXES THE REGION TO THE DOMAINS OF THE FRANCS

MOYEN

| 7TH C. | 8TH C. | 9TH C. | 10TH C. |

CLOVIS, KING OF THE FRANCS, INVADE THE REGION

6TH C.

5TH C.

FALL OF THE ROMAN EMPIRE

DEVELOPMENT OF ABBEYS

WALLED CASTLES: BEGINNING OF FEUDALITY

VISIGOTHS INVADE THE REGION

4TH C.

ANTIQUITÉ

3RD C.

2

GALLO-ROMAN TIME, THE FIRST WALL IS BUILT

ARRIVAL OF CHRISTIANITY IN THE REGION

2ND C.

Can anyone help me out?

1ST C.

BIRTH OF CHRISTIANITY

JESUS-CHRIST

2

BIRTH OF CARCASO, GALLIC OPPIDUM

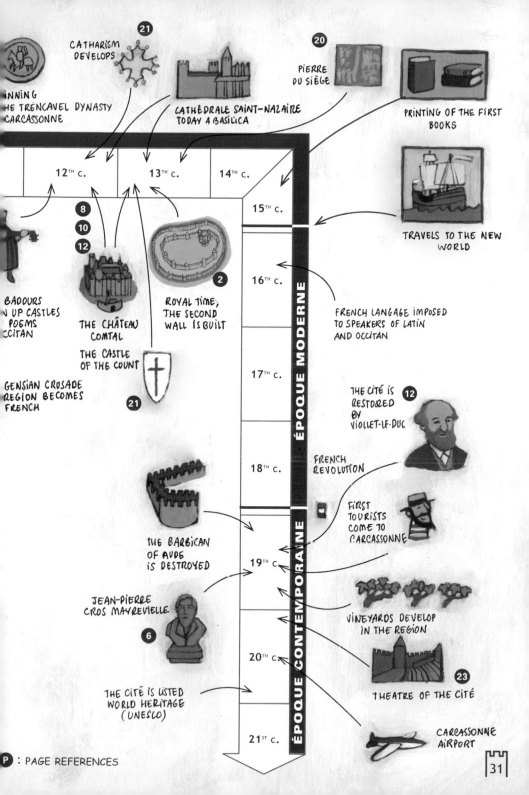

CATHARISM DEVELOPS 21

BEGINNING THE TRENCAVEL DYNASTY CARCASSONNE

CATHÉDRALE SAINT-NAZAIRE TODAY A BASILICA

PIERRE DU SIÈGE 20

PRINTING OF THE FIRST BOOKS

12TH C.

13TH C.

14TH C.

15TH C.

TRAVELS TO THE NEW WORLD

8
10
12

BADOURS UP CASTLES POEMS OCCITAN

THE CHÂTEAU COMTAL

THE CASTLE OF THE COUNT

2

ROYAL TIME, THE SECOND WALL IS BUILT

16TH C.

17TH C.

21

GENSIAN CROSADE REGION BECOMES FRENCH

ÉPOQUE MODERNE

FRENCH LANGAGE IMPOSED TO SPEAKERS OF LATIN AND OCCITAN

THE CITÉ IS RESTORED BY VIOLLET-LE-DUC 12

18TH C.

FRENCH REVOLUTION

FIRST TOURISTS COME TO CARCASSONNE

THE BARBICAN OF AUDE IS DESTROYED

19TH C.

JEAN-PIERRE CROS MAYREVIELLE
6

ÉPOQUE CONTEMPORAINE

VINEYARDS DEVELOP IN THE REGION

20TH C.

THEATRE OF THE CITÉ 23

THE CITÉ IS LISTED WORLD HERITAGE (UNESCO)

21ST C.

CARCASSONNE AIRPORT

P : PAGE REFERENCES

31

FAISONS LA FÊTE À CARCASSONNE

THE TOWN IS RICH IN FESTIVALS AND EVENTS THROUGHOUT THE YEAR!

texts : Nathalie Louveau, Monique Subra-Jourdain

illustrations : Nathalie Louveau

CARCASSONNE BASTIDE,
CARCASSONNE CITÉ

Thanking Claude Marquié and Philippe Satgé for their help with the realization of the present work.

maquette : Mathieu Subra – traduction : Guillaume Subra

éditions du
Cabardès

© 2006 ÉDITIONS DU CABARDÈS,11610 Ventenac-Cabardès
Dépôt légal, 2ᵉ trimestre 2006. ISBN 2-9526802-0-5
Impression FRANCE QUERCY, Cahors

LA BASTIDE

outer wall

bastion

moat

bastion
Saint Martial

THE BASTIDE DURING THE 16TH C.

port

22 **24** **2**

square
André Chénier

21

BOULEVARD OMER SARRA

RUE DE LA LIBERTÉ

RUE ARMAGNAC

RUE DU 4 SEPTEMBRE

Canal du Midi

BOULEVARD DE VARSOVIE

RUE DES ÉTUDES

20 Église
Saint
Vincent

THE BASTIDE SAINT LOUIS (FRENCH
FOR A WALLED TOWN), WAS BUILT
IN 1620 ON THE ORDERS OF KING
SAINT LOUIS. IT WAS ENCIRCLED
WITH A WALL, AND PROTECTED WITH
TOWERS, THEN WITH BASTIONS
AND MOATS.

AS MOST OF THE BASTIDES,
THE TOWN IS DRAWN AS
A GRID. IT IS ORGANISED
AROUND THE PLACE CARNOT.

THE BASTIDE WAS THEN EXTEN-
DED TO PROGRESSIVELY BECOME
THE TOWN WE KNOW TODAY.
THE FORTIFICATIONS
WERE THEN DESTROYED.

THE MOATS, WHICH AT
THE TIME SERVED
AS A DUMPING GROUND, WERE
FILLED UP AND BECAME
THE BOULEVARDS.

A FEW REMAINS CAN STILL BE
FOUND TODAY, OUT OF WHICH
THE PORTAIL DES JACOBINS,
THREE BASTIONS, AND A FEW
TRACES OF WALLS NEAR THE
CATHÉDRALE SAINT MICHEL.

RUE DE LA RÉPUBLIQUE

RUE VICTOR HUGO

RUE DU Dr ALBERT TOMEY

RUE JULES SAUZÈDE

place
Carnot

16 **1**

RUE DE VERDUN

14

ma
de 1
Bou

BOULEVARD MARCOU

RUE LITTRÉ

chapelle des
Jésuites

RUE AIMÉ RAMOND

RUE CHARTRAN

RUE VOLTAIRE

cathédrale
St Michel

BOULEVARD BARBÈS

bastion
Calvaire

ruins
of the wall

P : PAGE REFERENCES

PLAN

Ready for the tour?
Ha ha! easy one!
LIBERTÉ
BOULEVARD JEAN JAURÈS
RUE JEAN BRINGER
RUE BARBÈS
Tourism information centre
DE VERDUN
musée des Beaux-Arts
square Gambetta
the river Aude
Pont-Neuf
28
lac de la Cavayère
12
RUE COSTE REBOULH
AIMÉ RAMOND
ROUTE DE NARBONNE
10
Pont-Vieux
Chapel Notre Dame de la Santé
BOULEVARD CAMILLE PELLETAN
4
RUE TRIVALLE
RUE VOLTAIRE
the Béal
église Saint Gimer
8
EVARD DU CDT ROUMENS
LA CITÉ
6
bastion Montmorency
the island
RUE DE LA BARBACANE
3

LA RUE TRIVALLE

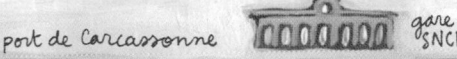

port de Carcassonne   gare SNCF

écluse   pont ma...

RUE TRIVALLE IS THE ANCIENT ROAD TO NARBONNE. THE SMALL COLOUR... HOUSES ARE KNOWN AS THE TRIVALLE DISTRICT. CAME THE BEGINNING OF ... 20TH CENTURY, IT WAS A REALLY POPULAR AREA. PEOPLE WOU... CHAT AWAY HAPPILY JUST OUTSIDE TH... HOUSES, WHILE WORKING FOR EXAMPLE ... THE RESEATING OF CHAIRS.

DEMAZEAU

MERCEDES PUJOL

VALDEVIÈVRE

79 L'OSTAL SIRVENTES

THIS ASSOCIATI... PROMOTES THE OCCIT... LANGUAGE, WHICH HAS BE... SPOKEN IN SOUTHERN FRA... CE FOR OVER A THOUSA... YEARS. THIS ALSO WAS T... LANGUAGE TROUBADOU... USED IN OUR REGION DURI... THE MIDDLE AGES.

56 LA MAISON DU CHEVALIER

IS A CONTEMPORARY ART GALLERY. FAMOUS ARTISTS ARE EXPOSED THERE. THEY COME FROM ALL SORTS OF COUNTRIES (RUSSIA, JAPAN, SPAIN, FRANCE, ...).
THE DIRECTOR OF THE GALLERY SELECTS THEM PATIENTLY AND LOVINGLY.

1 LA MANUFACTURE ROYALE

WAS BUILT IN 1696, ON THE ORDER OF KING LOUIS XIV. IT WAS A TEXTILE FACTORY, SPECIALISED IN WOOL: WASHING, CARDING, WEAVING, AND DYING.

4

101 - 105

THE FRESCO

EVERY LETTER OF CARCASSONNE IS REPRESENTED IN MIDDLE AGES ILLUSTRATION STYLE.

GET CLOSER AND DISCOVER SCENES OF THE HISTORY OF THE TOWN.

The letters are drawn juste like in Middle Ages books.

125 LA MAISON DES DUCS MONTMORENCY

IS A HALF-TIMBERED HOUSE. IN THE PAST, THEY WERE COATED TO PROTECT THE WOOD, SENSITIVE TO THE WEATHER.

L'ANCIENNE BARBACANE

L'ÉGLISE SAINT-GIMER

IS AT THE BOTTOM OF THE CITÉ, PLACE SAINT GIMER. IT CAN BE REACHED THROUGH THE RUE DE LA BARBACANE.

DESIGNED BY VIOLLET-LE-DUC, THE CHURCH WAS BUILT DURING THE 19TH CENTURY, JUST WHERE THE OLD BARBICAN OF THE PORTE D'AUDE WAS.

ITS HUMBLE ARCHITECTURE IS TO REMIND OF SAINT GIMER TO WHOM IT WAS DEDICATED. DESPITE BEING REALLY POOR, HE WOULD HAPPILY GIVE HIS BREAD TO THOSE IN NEED. AS A REWARD, HIS MOTHER SAW BEFORE HER EYES MULTIPLY THE BREADS SHE HAD JUST BAKED.

GO AROUND THE CHURCH AN TAKE THE COBBLED ROAD. AT THE BOTTOM OF THE CITÉ IS A LARGE MOUND FULL OF VEGETATION. FIGTREES GROW THERE ALONG WITH WILD LEAK BROOMS, DANDELIONS, AND ROCKET SALAD.

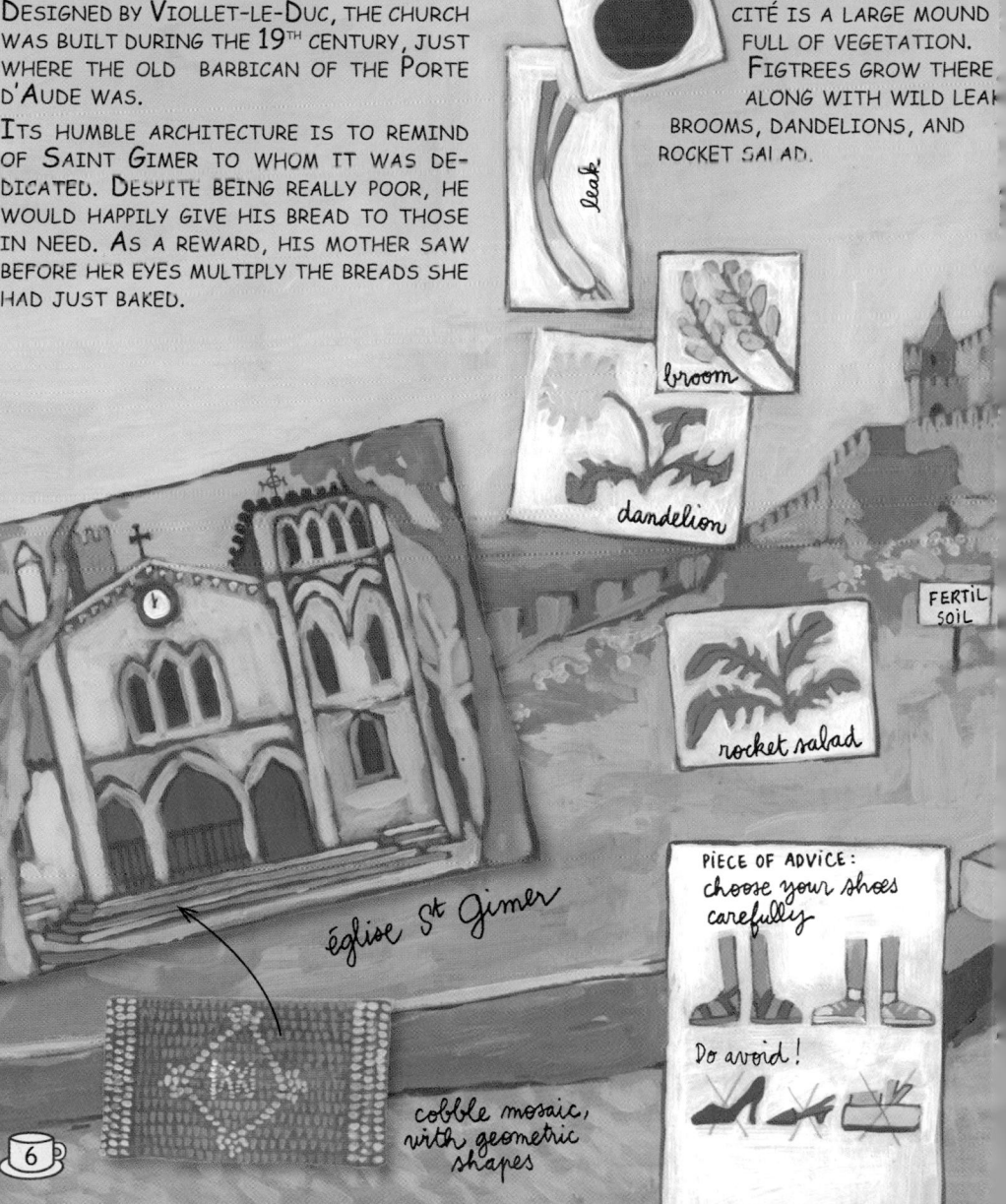

fig

leak

broom

dandelion

FERTIL SOIL

rocket salad

église St Gimer

cobble mosaic, with geometric shapes

PIECE OF ADVICE:
choose your shoes carefully

Do avoid !

6

écluse St Jean

al du midi

the walls

the Château Comtal

towards porte d'Aude (the second largest gate of the Cité)

The sun will soon set... Have your camera ready!

MANY A BATTLES TOOK PLACE HERE, BUT THOSE THAT ARE STILL REMEMBERED ARE THOSE THEY FOUGHT AS KIDS: CHILDREN OF THE CITÉ AGAINST CHILDREN OF THE TRIVALLE AND BARBACANE STREETS.

THEY WENT UP THE WALLS, WITH THEIR SLINGS AND WOODEN SWORDS... IT WOULD BE RATHER VIOLENT AT TIMES! BUT THESE BATTLES ALWAYS HAD THEIR HAPPY ENDINGS. AND HENCE WERE CONTINUALLY REVIVED THE HISTORY AND THE STORIES OF THE PORTE D'AUDE...

7

L'ÎLE AU PIED DU PONT-VIEUX

IN THIS PART OF THE TOWN, YOU CAN HAVE A STROLL OR TOUR AROUND ON YOUR BIKE, YOU CAN RUN ABOUT, HAVE FUN ON THE SPORTS FACILITIES OF THE RUNNING TRACK AND FEEL ALL SPORTY, OR MAYBE YOU'LL JUST ENJOY HAVING A REST BY THE RIVERSIDE.

le pont vieux

jardin Bellevue
(with a nice view on the Cité)

ford

barrage du Païcherou

the river Aude

That way are nice strolls along the river

the béal

squi

camp-site of the Cité

8

écluse double
du Fresquel

écluse simple
du Fresquel

canal du midi

the walk by the Béal

OUAF OUAF

OUAF ARF

fish

coypu

Bip Bip Bip
Bip

Bip

heron

You may also eat acacia
flowers during spring, or take
a close look at the borders
of the river: there are
often ducks asleep,
coypus, or a heron wai-
ting for his meal to pass by...

Listen carefully and you may
hear a donkey bray, and looking back, you'll get a different perspective on
the Cité...

duck

LE PONT-VIEUX

LE PONT-VIEUX (AULD BRIDGE) WAS BUILT DURING THE 14TH CENTURY. UP TO THE 19TH CENTURY, IT WAS THE ONLY WAY BETWEEN THE CITÉ AND THE BASTIDE.

CARCASSONNE IS SPLIT INTO TWO BY THE RIVER AUDE, AND THIS GEOGRAPHIC SEPARATION HAS FOR A LONG TIME DIVIDED THE INHABITANTS : THOSE OF THE UPPER TOWN (THE CITÉ, ON THE HILLS) AND THOSE OF THE LOWER TOWN (THE BASTIDE SAINT LOUIS AND ITS DISTRICT).

THE VIEW FROM THE BRIDGE OVER THE CITÉ IS TRULY AMAZING!

EVERY YEAR SINCE 1898, ON JULY THE 14TH, THE CITÉ RE-ENACTS THE TIME OF THE SIEGE. THE FIREWORKS THAT TAKE PLACE ALWAYS END WITH A SPECTACULAR CRIMSONING OF THE CITÉ. THOUSANDS OF PEOPLE ATTEND THE EVENT EVERY SUMMER. CAREFUL NOT TO LOSE A SHOE OR YOUR HAT IN THE CROWD!

dayly jogging of the military forces

HOP HOP HOP

HOP HOP HOP HOP

BIP BIP BIP BIP

the Béal

écluse de l'Évêque

canal du midi

A « GIANT METRE » MEASURES THE LEVELS OF THE WATER DURING FLOODS. YOU MAY SEE FOR EXAMPLE THE HEIGHT WATER REACHED IN 1891.

Chapel Notre Dame de la Santé

THE BRIDGE FEATURES MANY « BEAKS », WHICH BREAK THE WAVES OF THE RIVER. HIS IS ALSO WHERE PEOPLE WOULD GO TO VE WAY TO THE CHARIOTS.

« Portrait de Madame Astre »
Achille Laugé (1861 - 1944), Audois painter

« Portrait de Fabre d'Eglantine »
Pierre - Augustin Thomire, 18ᵀᴴ c.

FABRE IS KNOWN FOR HIS PARTICIPATION TO REWRITIN THE REPUBLICAN CALENDAR. DURING THE FRENCH REVOLU TION, DAYS AND MONTHS HA BEEN RENAMED.

THIS POET, BORN IN CARCASSONNE, IS ALSO FAMOUS FOR A FRENCH LULLABY:

It feels like her eyes are following me when I move!

Oh! And look! There are plenty of colourful dashes!

IL PLEUT IL PLEUT BERGÈRE RENTRE TES BLANCS MOUTONS!

« Choc de Cavalerie », Jacques Gameli (1738 - 1803), Audois painter

« Les emmurés de Carcassonne »
Jean - Paul Laurens (1838 - 1921)

THIS LARGE PAINTING SHOWS MONK BERNARD DÉLICIEUX. HE IS DEFENDING MEN ACCUSED OF CATHAR HERESY DOMINICAN BROTHERS KEEP IN THE DE LA MURE PRISON.

EUGENE POUBEL

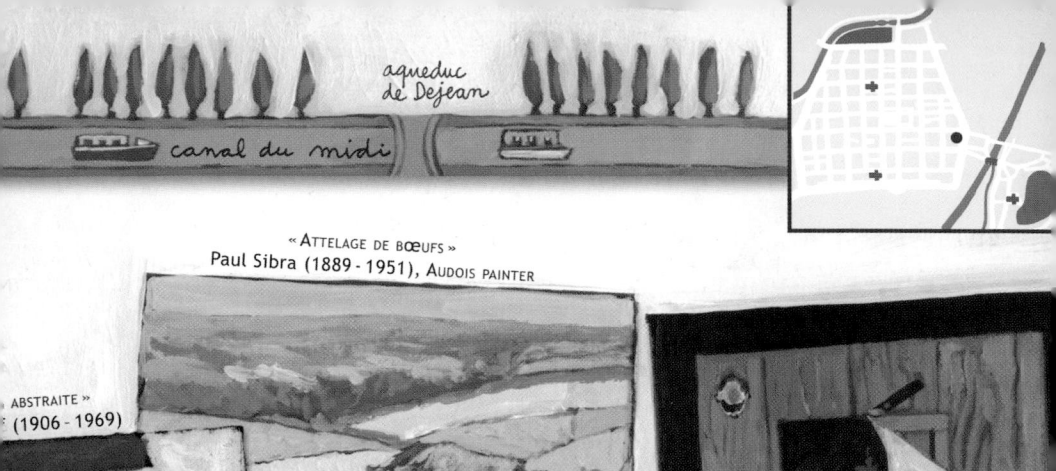

« ATTELAGE DE BŒUFS »
Paul Sibra (1889 - 1951), AUDOIS PAINTER

ABSTRAITE »
(1906 - 1969)

« NATURE MORTE EN TROMPE L'ŒIL »
Cornélius Norbertus Gysbrecht,
17TH C.

HE PERMANENT EXHIBITION:

N THE FIRST FLOOR WORKS OF THE 18TH AND 19TH CENTURIES ARE DISPLAYED.

N THE GROUND FLOOR MORE MODERN 20TH CENTURY PAINTINGS AND SCULPTURES CAN BE FOUND.

HE MUSEUM ORGANISES ALSO TEMPORARY EXHIBITIONS THREE TIMES A YEAR.

TTLE KNOWN FACT

N THE INNER YARD OF THE MUSEUM IS THE BUST OF EUGÈNE POU-
LLE (1831-1907). IN 1883, THEN PREFECT OF PARIS, HE ORDERED
E USE OF A LARGE RECEPTACLE WITH HANDLES TO GATHER GARBAGE.
HESE WERE FORMERLY SIMPLY THROWN DIRECTLY IN THE STREET!
NS WHERE HENCEFORTH CALLED IN FRANCE
TER HIS CREATOR: « POUBELLES »!

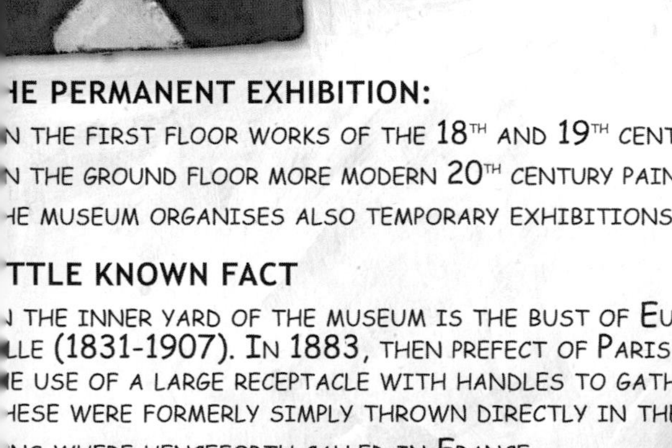

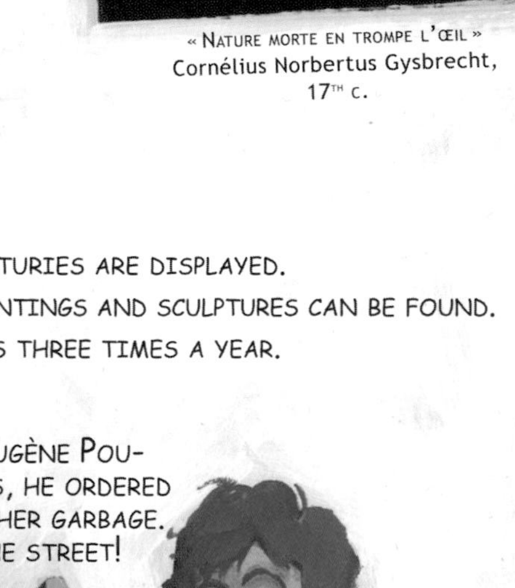

LA RUE DE VERDUN

LES HALLES

ARE SITUATED BETWEEN THE RUE DE VERDUN AND THE RUE AIMÉ RAMOND, AND DATE BACK FROM THE 18TH CENTURY. THEY WOULD BE USED BY BUTCHERS, THE POIDS DU ROY, GRAIN MEASURERS, SECURITY GUARDS, AND THE BUREAU OF THE EQUIVALENT (TAX ON MEAT, FISH AND WINE).

the halls today

cheesemongers

fishery

butchery

former hall for poultry (19th c.)

former hall for butchery (18 c.)

former hall for grains (18 c.)

LE PILORI

THIS IS WHERE THIEVES WERE EXPOSED. FROM 11 AM T NOON, PEOPLE COULD INSULT THEM OR THRO ALL SORT OF NASTY THINGS AT THEM...

So what exactly is the King's weight?

It's actually no particular weight! It was where all goods had to be weighted.

14

LA MAISON JOE BOUSQUET

(ALSO KNOWN AS «LA MAISON DES MÉMOIRES»)

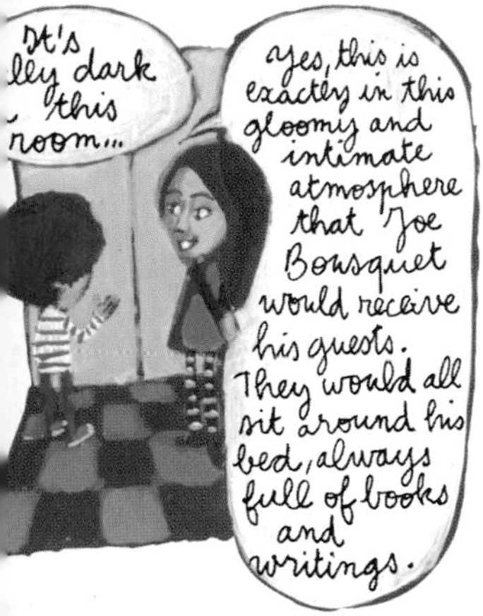

JOE BOUSQUET, POET AND WRITER, WAS DISABLED. IN HIS ROOM, THE SHUTTERS WERE CONSISTENTLY CLOSED, AND THE WALLS COVERED WITH PAINTINGS OF GREAT REKNOWN (ERNST, DALI, MAGRITTE, MIRO...). HE RECEIVED THERE ARTISTS, WRITERS AND POETS, SUCH AS PAUL ELUARD, ANDRÉ GIDE, ARAGON, OR EVEN PHILOSOPHERS LIKE SIMONE WEIL.

It's lly dark this room...

Yes, this is exactly in this gloomy and intimate atmosphere that Joe Bousquet would receive his guests. They would all sit around his bed, always full of books and writings.

ROUGH A FRENCH WINDOW IS HIS ROOM, KEPT AS WAS WHEN JOE BOUSQUET LIVED IN IT.

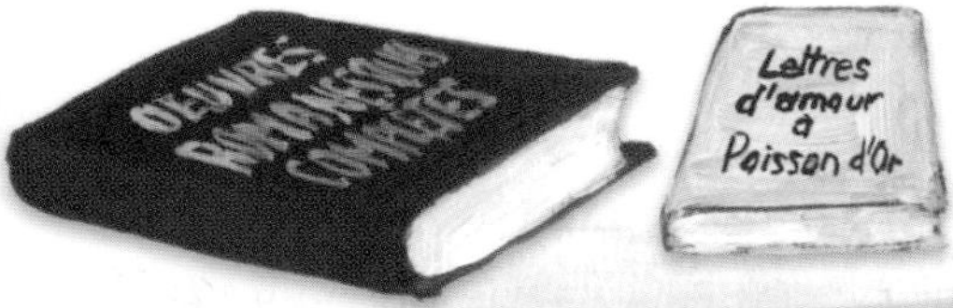

OEUVRES ROMANESQUES COMPLÈTES

Lettres d'amour à Poisson d'Or

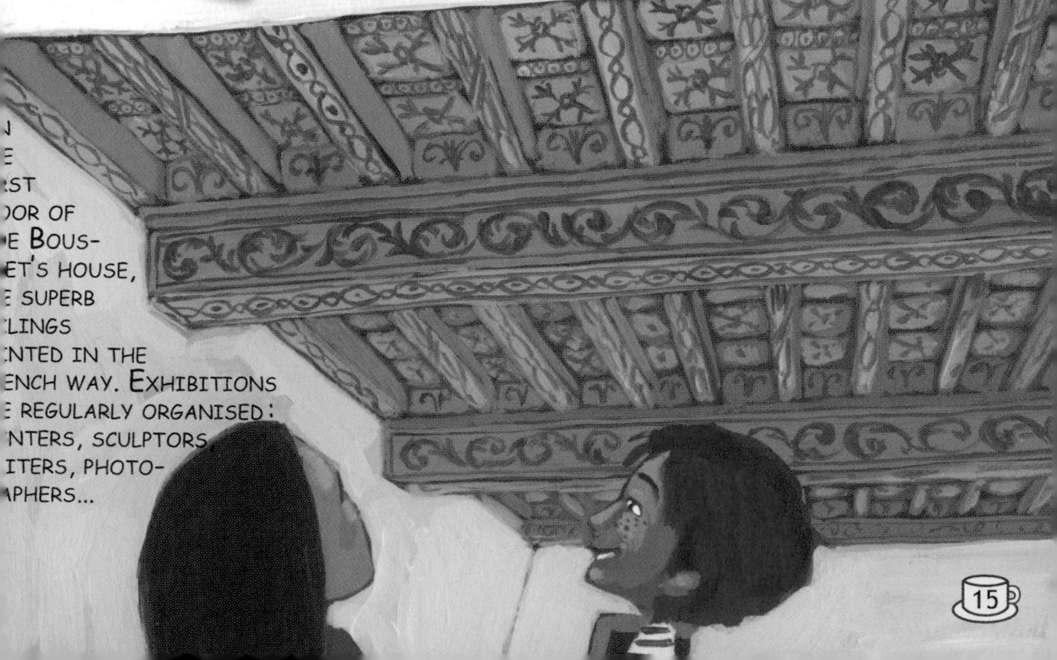

Joe Bousquet (1897 - 1950)

J E ST OR OF E BOUS- ET'S HOUSE, E SUPERB LINGS NTED IN THE ENCH WAY. EXHIBITIONS E REGULARLY ORGANISED : NTERS, SCULPTORS ITERS, PHOTO- APHERS...

15

LA PLACE CARNOT

écluse de Trèbes

Neptune's fountain lays at the centre of the place Carnot. It is composed of various elements linked to water: in addition to the Roman god of the seas, Neptune, naiads, tritons and dolphins can be spotted.

The fountain was sculpted during the 18TH century by the Italians Barata, father and son.

LITTLE KNOWN FACT

One day, wine flowed out of the fountain. Water had been replaced for the coming of the Duke of Orleans in 1839.

Neptune, God of the seas

Naiad

Triton

dolphin

incarnate marble, from Caunes-Minervois

LOCAL WE
IN CARCASSONNE
"MAUVAIS" MEANS
"MAUVAIS" ALSO M
WINDY (SPECIA
WIND BLOWS NC
STICKY!). AND
"MAUVAIS" W
REFERENCE
RAIN, BUT FO
WEATHER
IS THE O

aqueduc
millegrand

nal du midi

E PLACE CARNOT IS THE MAIN PLACE
THE TOWN. ORIGINALLY A LOT LAR-
IT WAS SURROUNDED BY COVERED
LS.

ERE WERE ALSO FOUNTAINS AT
CH CORNER, AND IF YOU LOOK
WN CLOSELY, THE GROUND IS
DE OF MARBLE.

This is what the Place Carnot must
have looked like before the fire of 1622.

THE PLACE CARNOT IS
ONE OF THE FAVOURITE
PLACES FOR CARCAS-
SONNAIS. IT IS RATHER
TYPICAL OF SOUTHERN FRANCE:
PLANE TREES, COFFEE SHOPS,
AND TERRACES THAT ALWAYS
FILL UP AS SOON AS THE
SUN IS OUT, EVEN IN
THE HEART OF
THE WINTER.

NOT TO BE MISSED, IN THE TWO
CHOCOLATE MAKERS OF THE PLACE

CANNONBALLS
OF THE CITÉ

THE FAMOUS
KOUGLOF

AND AT THE BAKER'S ON THE STREET
VICTOR HUGO
THE "COBBLES"
(Sweets)

17

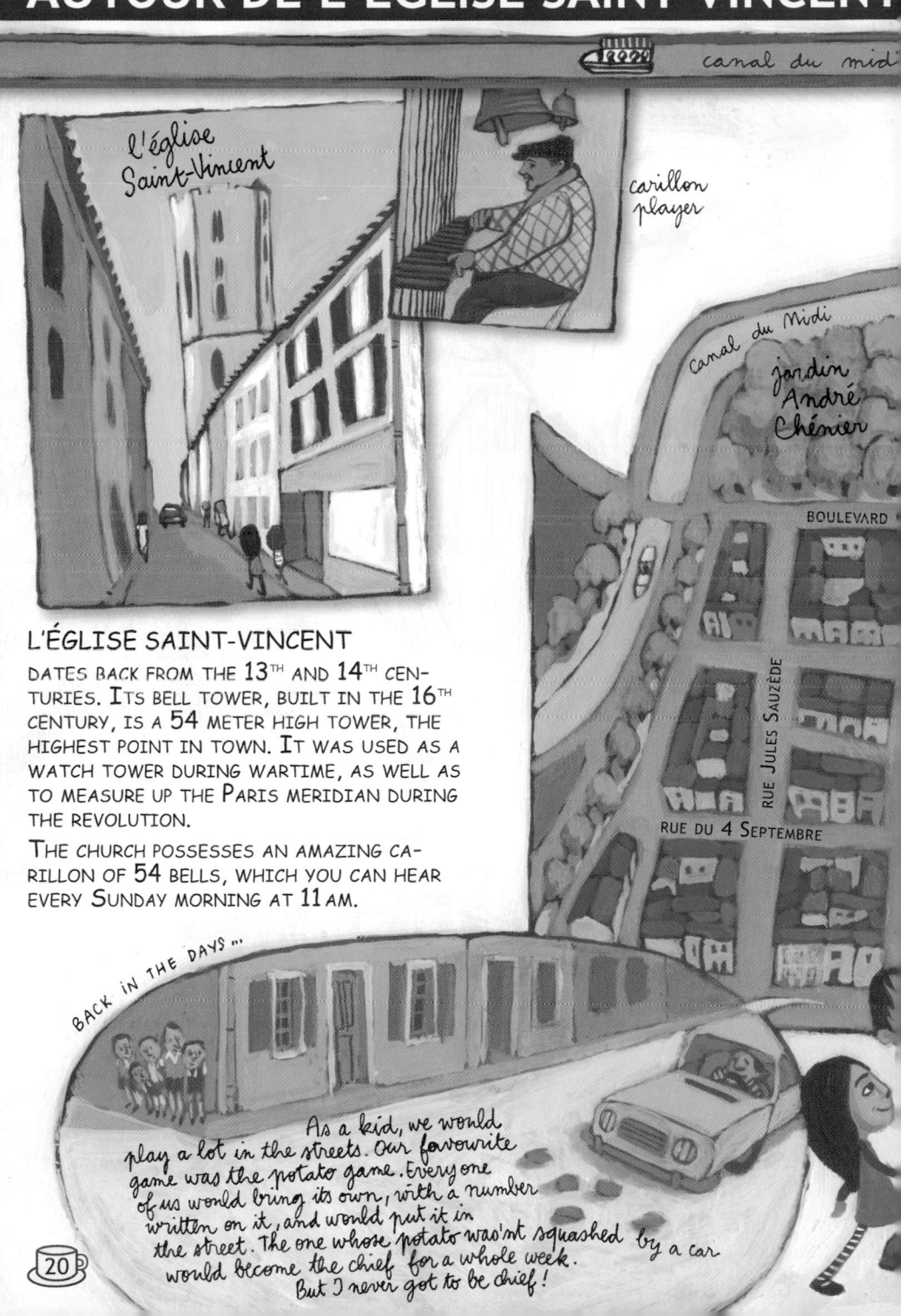

canal du midi

l'église Saint-Vincent

carillon player

Canal du Midi

Jardin André Chénier

BOULEVARD

RUE JULES SAUZÈDE

RUE DU 4 Septembre

L'ÉGLISE SAINT-VINCENT

DATES BACK FROM THE 13TH AND 14TH CENTURIES. ITS BELL TOWER, BUILT IN THE 16TH CENTURY, IS A 54 METER HIGH TOWER, THE HIGHEST POINT IN TOWN. IT WAS USED AS A WATCH TOWER DURING WARTIME, AS WELL AS TO MEASURE UP THE PARIS MERIDIAN DURING THE REVOLUTION.

THE CHURCH POSSESSES AN AMAZING CARILLON OF 54 BELLS, WHICH YOU CAN HEAR EVERY SUNDAY MORNING AT 11 AM.

BACK IN THE DAYS "..

As a kid, we would play a lot in the streets. Our favourite game was the potato game. Everyone of us would bring its own, with a number written on it, and would put it in the street. The one whose potato was'nt squashed by a car would become the chief for a whole week. But I never got to be chief!

JARDIN ANDRÉ CHÉNIER

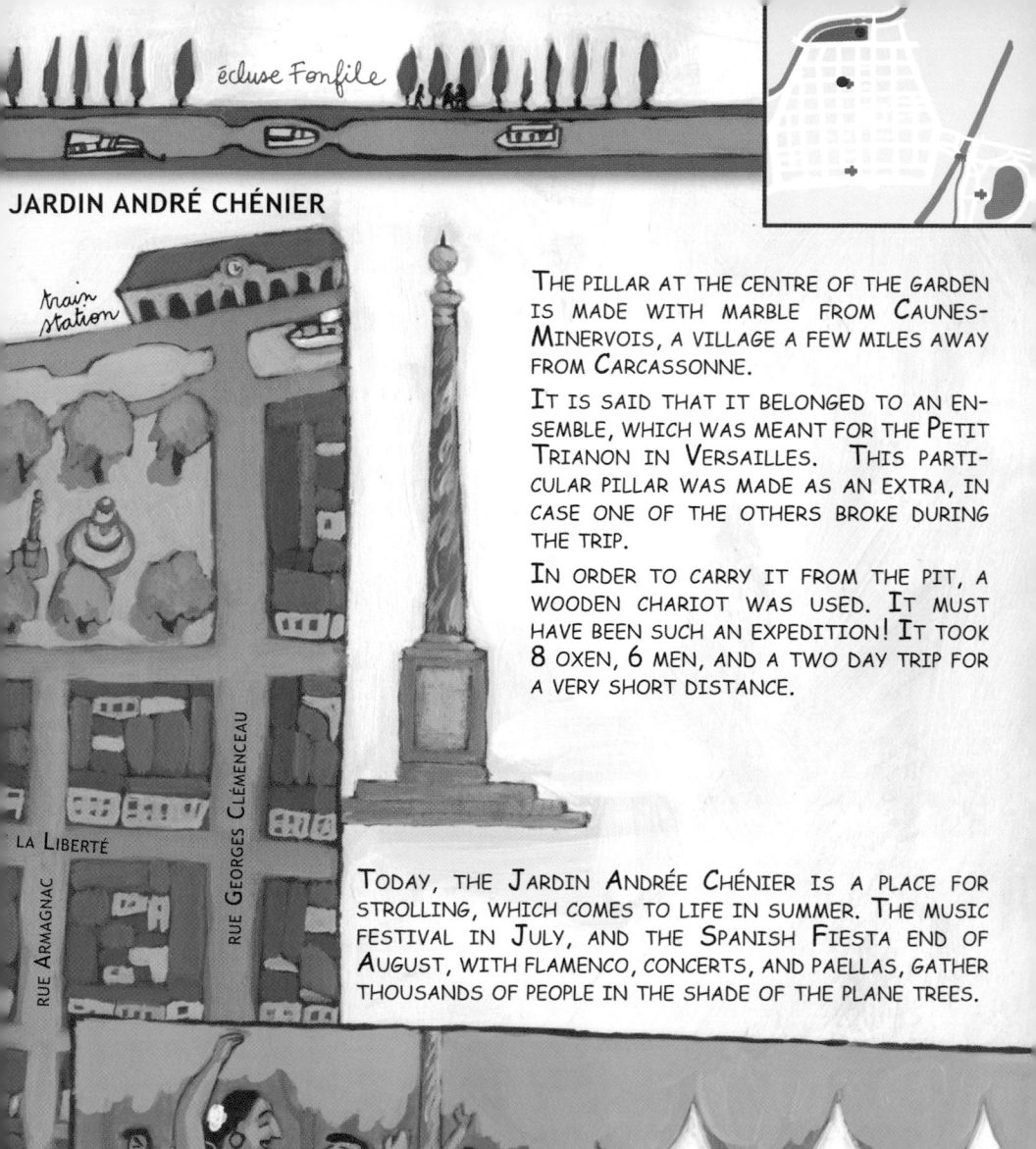

train station

LA LIBERTÉ

RUE GEORGES CLÉMENCEAU

RUE ARMAGNAC

THE PILLAR AT THE CENTRE OF THE GARDEN IS MADE WITH MARBLE FROM CAUNES-MINERVOIS, A VILLAGE A FEW MILES AWAY FROM CARCASSONNE.

IT IS SAID THAT IT BELONGED TO AN ENSEMBLE, WHICH WAS MEANT FOR THE PETIT TRIANON IN VERSAILLES. THIS PARTICULAR PILLAR WAS MADE AS AN EXTRA, IN CASE ONE OF THE OTHERS BROKE DURING THE TRIP.

IN ORDER TO CARRY IT FROM THE PIT, A WOODEN CHARIOT WAS USED. IT MUST HAVE BEEN SUCH AN EXPEDITION! IT TOOK 8 OXEN, 6 MEN, AND A TWO DAY TRIP FOR A VERY SHORT DISTANCE.

TODAY, THE JARDIN ANDRÉE CHÉNIER IS A PLACE FOR STROLLING, WHICH COMES TO LIFE IN SUMMER. THE MUSIC FESTIVAL IN JULY, AND THE SPANISH FIESTA END OF AUGUST, WITH FLAMENCO, CONCERTS, AND PAELLAS, GATHER THOUSANDS OF PEOPLE IN THE SHADE OF THE PLANE TREES.

LE CANAL DU MIDI

écluse St Martin

THE HISTORY BEHIND IT

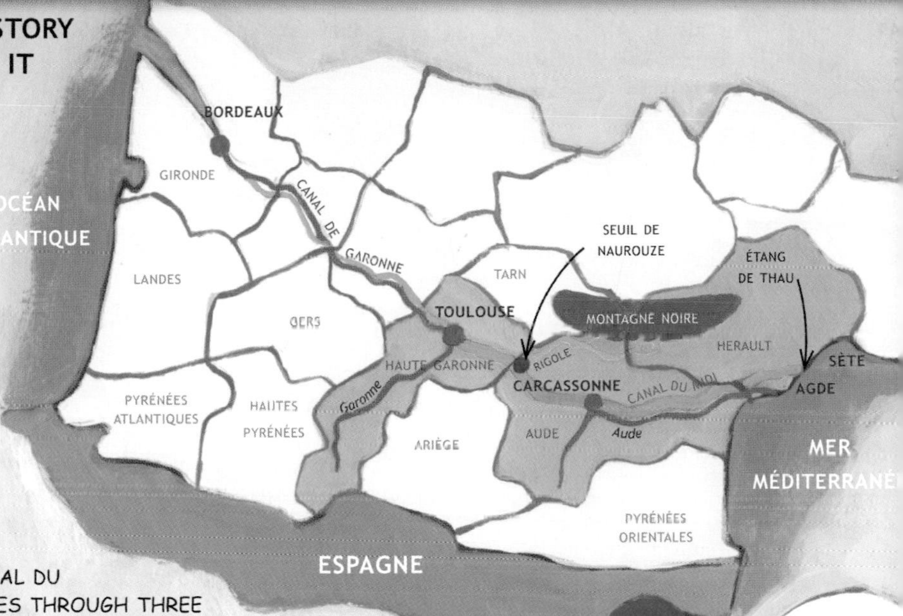

OCÉAN ATLANTIQUE

BORDEAUX

GIRONDE

CANAL DE GARONNE

LANDES

GERS

TARN

TOULOUSE

HAUTE-GARONNE

RIGOLE

Garonne

HAUTES PYRÉNÉES

PYRÉNÉES ATLANTIQUES

ARIÈGE

ESPAGNE

SEUIL DE NAUROUZE

MONTAGNE NOIRE

ÉTANG DE THAU

HERAULT

SÈTE

CARCASSONNE

CANAL DU MIDI

AGDE

AUDE

Aude

PYRÉNÉES ORIENTALES

MER MÉDITERRANÈ

THE CANAL DU MIDI GOES THROUGH THREE DÉPARTEMENTS, THE ADMINISTRATIVE DIVISIONS OF FRANCE. IT WAS BUILT IN THE 17TH CENTURY BY PIERRE PAUL RIQUET, WHO PUT IN IT HIS PERSONAL MONEY. IT WAS THEN CALLED CANAL ROYAL DE LANGUEDOC.

IT TOOK 15 YEARS OF HARD WORK (1666-1681). RIQUET'S IDEA WAS TO BRIDGE THE ATLANTIC OCEAN TO THE MEDITERRANEAN SEA, BUILDING A CANAL BETWEEN THE MEDITERANEAN AND THE RIVER GARONNE. THAT WAY, BOATS WOULD NO LONGER NEED TO GO AROUND SPAIN. THERE WAS NOT ONLY ECONOMIC BUT ALSO POLITIC INTEREST AT STAKE.

THE CANAL DU LANGUEDOC WOULD LATER ON BE EXTENDED WITH ANOTHER CANAL, PARALLEL TO THE RIVER GARONNE IN 1856.

It took 12,000 men to undertake this enormous project!

PIERRE PAUL RIQUET (1604-1680)

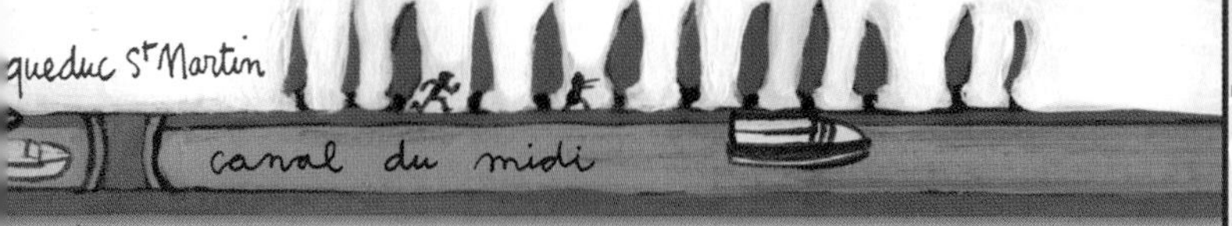
queduc St Martin
canal du midi

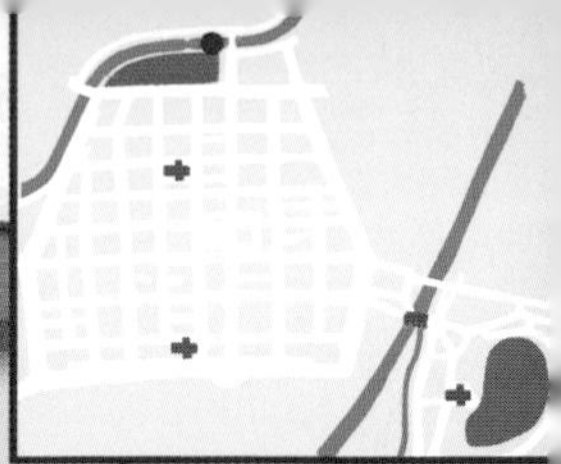

ATER HAD TO BE BROUGHT TO THE CANAL. RIQUET HAD THE IDEA OF GANISING A COMPLEX SYSTEM OF CHANNELS AND TRENCHES FROM THE ONTAGNE NOIRE. USING THE SEUIL DE NAUROUZE (PASS OF NAU-UZE), THE HIGHEST POINT OF THE CANAL, WATER WOULD GO DOWN THE GARONNE ON ONE SIDE AND TO THE MEDITERANNEAN ON THE HER.

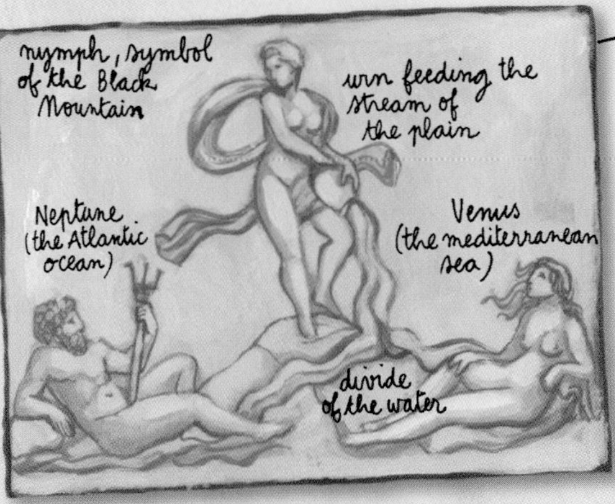
nymph, symbol of the Black Mountain
urn feeding the stream of the plain
Neptune (the Atlantic ocean)
Venus (the mediterranean sea)
divide of the water

EMBOSSED DESIGN, SYMBOLISING THE MONTAGNE NOIRE

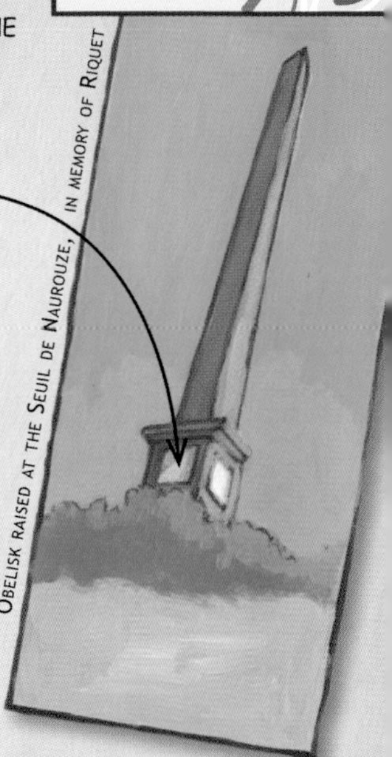

OBELISK RAISED AT THE SEUIL DE NAUROUZE, IN MEMORY OF RIQUET

THE OLD DAYS, THE ECONOMIC INTEREST OF THE CANAL S ESSENTIAL. IT WAS USED TO CARRY GOODS ON BARGES: EALS, WINE, PASTEL...

TILL THE 19TH CENTURY, BARGES DID NOT USE MOTORS. TO TRACK THEM, RSES OR MULES WERE USED, WHICH WOULD USE THE TOWING ROAD. TRACES THE ROPES USED ARE STILL VISIBLE ON SOME STONES.

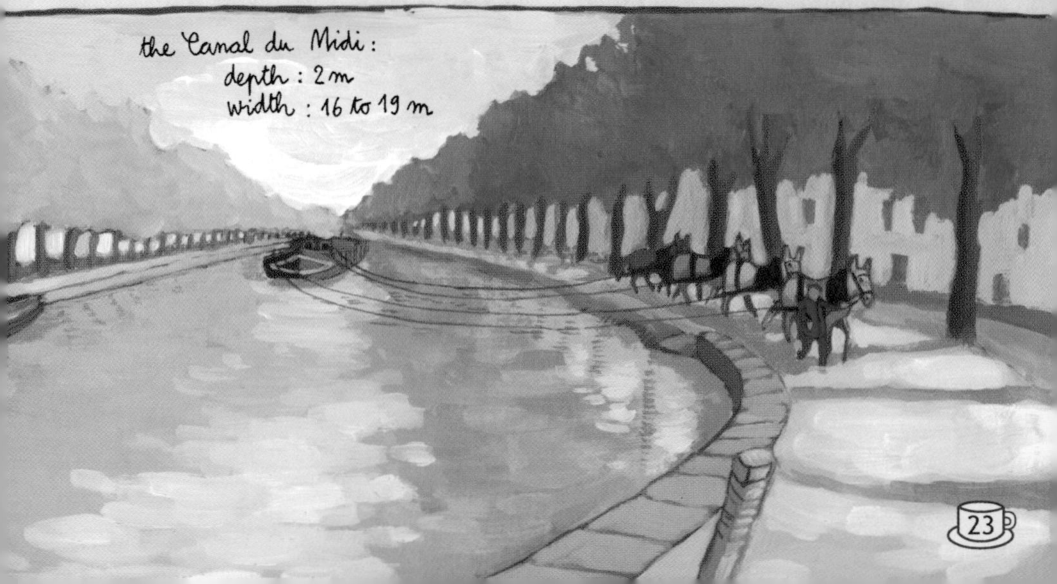
the Canal du Midi :
depth : 2m
width : 16 to 19 m

ITS LOCKS

THE CANAL HAS 63 LOCKS. THEY WERE USED TO GO UP THE RIVER DESPITE THE DIFFERENCES LEVEL. THAT WAY, BARGES COULD NAVIGATE ON A STILL RIVER.

THE PRINCIPLE OF THE LOCKS IS RATHER SIMPLE. THE BASIN WOULD BE EMPTIED OR FILLED HENCE ALLOWING THE BARGES TO KEEP ON GOING.

ACCORDING TO THE DIFFERENCE OF HEIGHT, UP TO THREE OR FOUR LOCKS ARE USED.

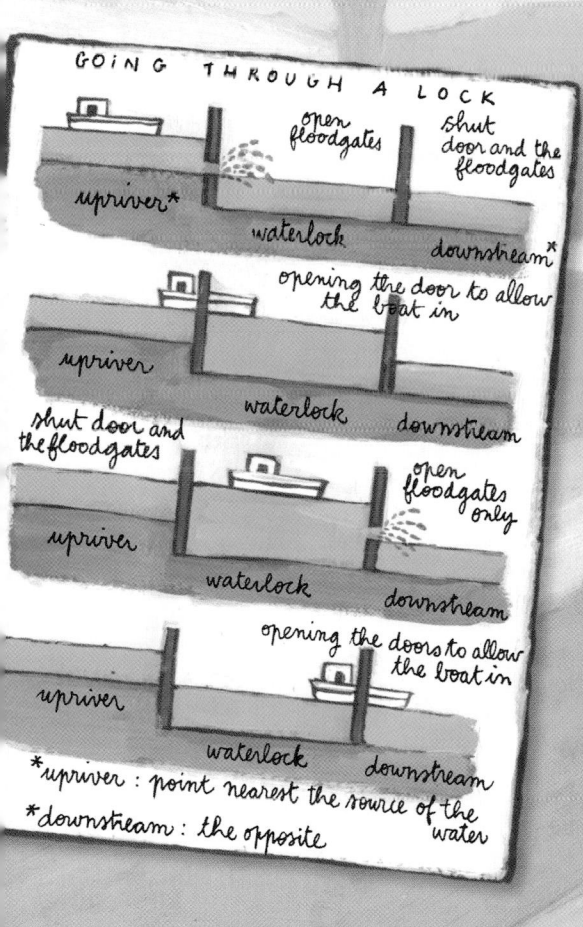

GOING THROUGH A LOCK

open floodgates — shut door and the floodgates

upriver*

waterlock — downstream*

opening the door to allow the boat in

upriver

waterlock — downstream

shut door and the floodgates

open floodgates only

upriver

waterlock — downstream

opening the doors to allow the boat in

upriver

waterlock — downstream

*upriver : point nearest the source of the water
*downstream : the opposite

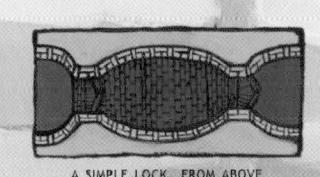

A SIMPLE LOCK, FROM ABOVE

THE ALMOND LIKE SHAPE IS CHARACTER[IS]TIC OF THE CANAL DU MIDI. IT ALLO[WS] THE PRESSURE ON THE RIVERSIDES TO [BE] DIVIDED ON THE WALLS, AND MORE TH[AN] ONE BOAT CAN THUS USE THE LOCK AT T[HE] SAME TIME.

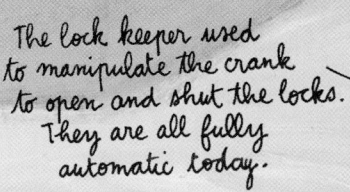

house of the lock keeper

the lock keeper

The lock keeper used to manipulate the crank to open and shut the locks. They are all fully automatic today.

24

THE CANAL DU MIDI HAS BEEN ADDED TO THE UNESCO* LIST OF WORLD HERITAGE IN 1997. THE CITÉ IS ALSO ON THE UNESCO LIST.

When the canal crosses another river, it uses a special bridge: "pont-canal". Outside Carcassonne, towards Conques, in "le Pont Rouge", you may see one from near.

*NESCO: UNITED NATION EDUCATION, SCIENCE AND CULTURE ORGANISATION

LE CANAL DU MIDI

aqueduc Ribausset

WALKING BY THE CANAL

WHEN THE CANAL DU MIDI WAS BUILT TREES WERE PLANTED ON THE RIVERSIDE: FIGTREES, OLIVETREES, AND WEEPING WILLOWS. THEIR ROOTS WERE DAMAGED HOWEVER WITH THE PASSING OF HORSES ON THE TOWING WAY. THEY WERE THUS REPLACED BY PLANE TREES AND CYPRESSES, WHICH ROOTS ARE STRONGER.

plane tree

The maximum speed allowed is 8 km/h.

LITTLE KNOWN FACT

THE BOAT TRIP TO THE ATLANTIC OCEAN FROM CARCASSONNE IS 1 DAYS LONG, AND IT TAKES 5 DAY TO REACH THE MEDITERRANEAN SEA.

aqueduc argent double

canal du midi

cypress

THE CANAL DU MIDI TO-
DAY IS A QUIET PLACE FOR
CRUISES, ONLY PUNCTUA-
TED BY LOCKS. WHEN
THE BOAT STOPS, IT'S
AN EXCELLENT OP-
PORTUNITY TO WALK
AROUND AND DISCOVER
THE TOWNS AND VIL-
LAGES, AND MAYBE TRY
SOME LOCAL FOOD...

vine

I'm sure I can cycle as fast as a barge on the canal!

OU MAY CHOOSE TO TAKE A BOAT
N THE CANAL, OR A BICYCLE ON
HE TOWING WAY! A FRIENDLY
DVICE THOUGH... YOU'D BE BEST
AKING THE ROAD GOING TO THE
EDITERRANEAN SEA, AS THIS
AD GOES DOWN!

27

LE LAC DE LA CAVAYÈRE

écluse Jouarres

canal du midi

fountain

AROUND THE LAKE, THE VEGETATION IS TYPICALLY MEDITERRANEAN.

PINES AND GREEN OAKS GROW THERE, BOTH OF WHICH KEEPING THEIR LEAVES DURING THE WINTER, AS WELL AS THYME, A VERY FRAGRANT PLANT, AND DURING SPRING TIME, ORCHIDS (WHICH SHOULD NOT BE PICKED AS THEY ARE A PROTECTED SPECIE).

the birds' island
(where they come
and nest)

miniature
golf

emergency tent
(a lifeguard watches
over the swimmers)

BIRTH OF ISLAM

MOYEN ÂGE

	7TH C.	8TH C.	9TH C.	10TH C.	11TH C.
6TH C.					

FALL OF THE ROMAN EMPIRE

DEVELOPMENT OF ABBEYS

WALLED CASTLES: BEGINNING OF THE FEUDALITY

5TH C.

FALL OF THE ROMAN EMPIRE

4TH C.

ANTIQUITÉ

3RD C. — ✝ ARRIVAL OF CHRISTIANITY IN THE REGION

2ND C.

1ST C. — ✝ BIRTH OF CHRISTIANITY

JESUS CHRIST

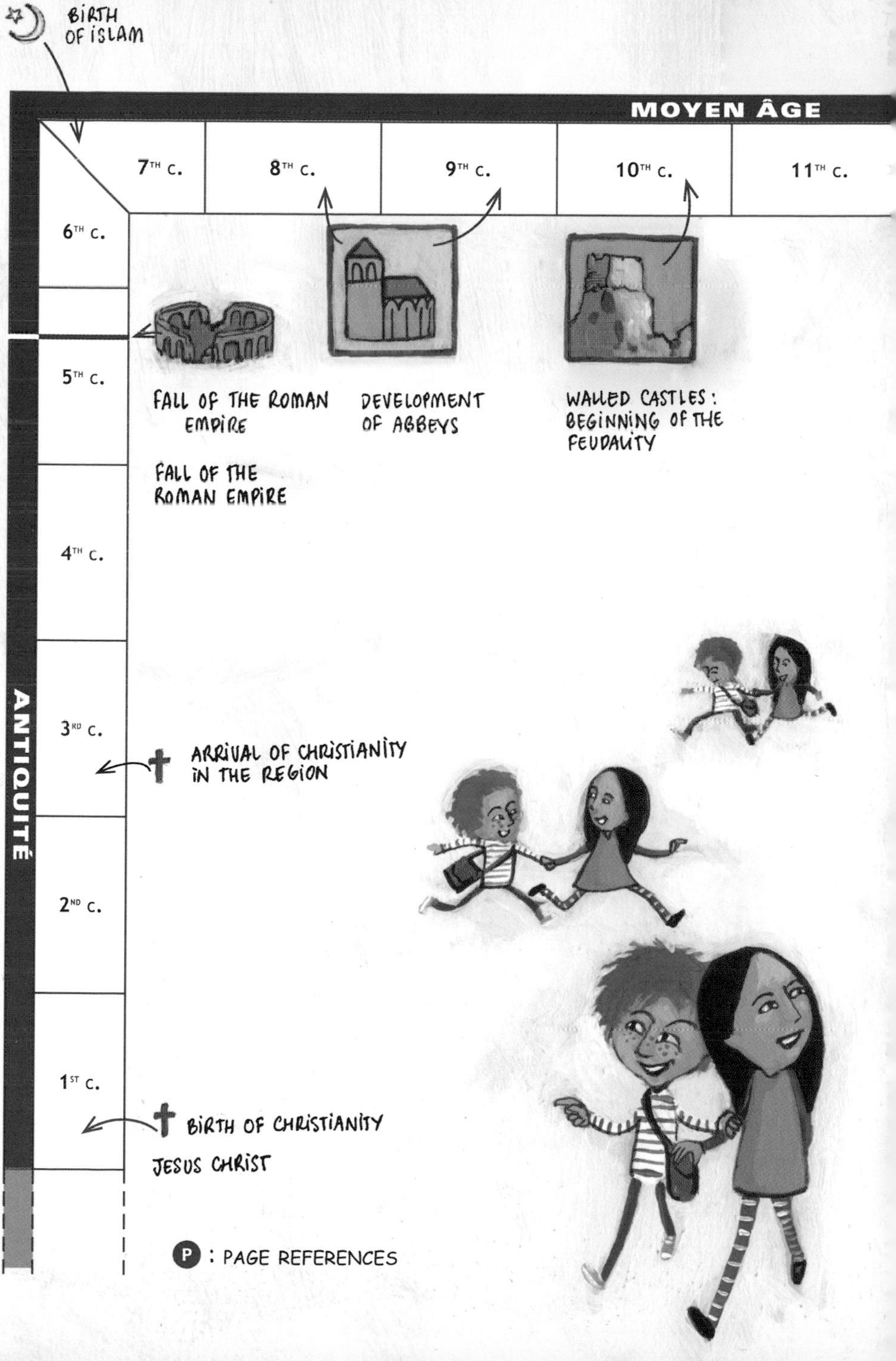

P : PAGE REFERENCES

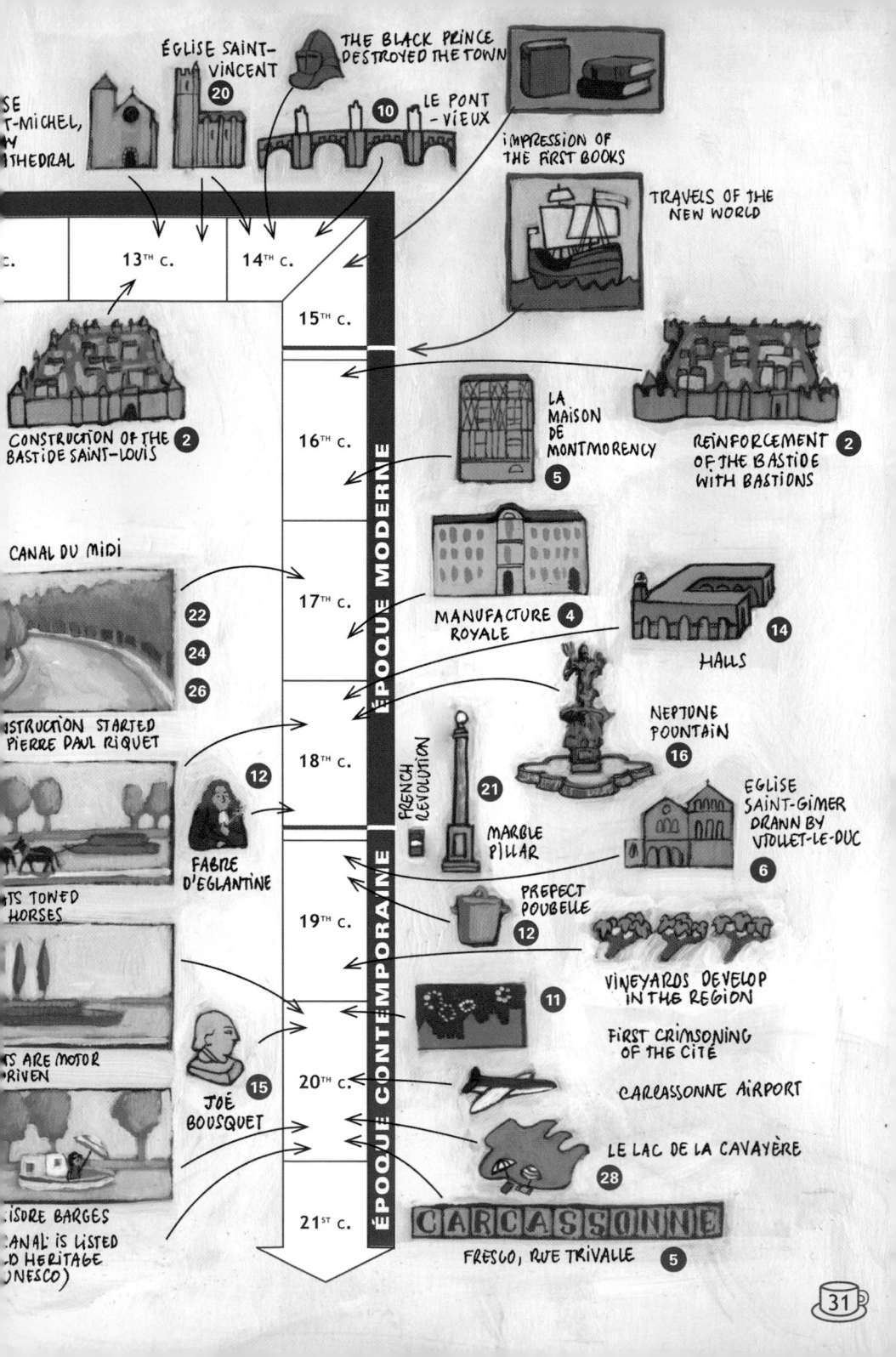

E T-MICHEL, CATHEDRAL

ÉGLISE SAINT-VINCENT **20**

THE BLACK PRINCE DESTROYED THE TOWN

LE PONT-VIEUX **10**

IMPRESSION OF THE FIRST BOOKS

TRAVELS OF THE NEW WORLD

13TH C.

14TH C.

15TH C.

CONSTRUCTION OF THE BASTIDE SAINT-LOUIS **2**

16TH C.

LA MAISON DE MONTMORENCY **5**

REINFORCEMENT OF THE BASTIDE WITH BASTIONS **2**

ÉPOQUE MODERNE

CANAL DU MIDI

22
24
26

ISTRUCTION STARTED PIERRE PAUL RIQUET

17TH C.

MANUFACTURE ROYALE **4**

HALLS **14**

NEPTUNE FOUNTAIN **16**

18TH C.

FABRE D'ÉGLANTINE **12**

FRENCH REVOLUTION

MARBLE PILLAR **21**

ÉGLISE SAINT-GIMER DRAWN BY VIOLLET-LE-DUC **6**

TS TOWED HORSES

19TH C.

PREFECT POUBELLE **12**

VINEYARDS DEVELOP IN THE REGION **11**

FIRST CRIMSONING OF THE CITÉ

TS ARE MOTOR RIVEN

JOË BOUSQUET **15**

20TH C.

CARCASSONNE AIRPORT

ÉPOQUE CONTEMPORAINE

LE LAC DE LA CAVAYÈRE **28**

ISDRE BARGES

CANAL IS LISTED D HERITAGE UNESCO)

21ST C.

CARCASSONNE

FRESCO, RUE TRIVALLE **5**

31